ABOUT THE THREE LINES THAT STRIKE KEY POINTS

AN EXPLANATION OF THOROUGH CUT WITH DIRECT CROSSING WOVEN IN BY DODRUPCHEN III TENPA'I NYIMA

TONY DUFF
PADMA KARPO TRANSLATION COMMITTEE

This text is secret and should not be shown to those who have not had the necessary introduction and instructions of the Thorough Cut system of Dzogchen meditation. If you have not had the necessary instructions, reading this text can be harmful to your spiritual health! Seal. Seal. Seal.

First edition, February 2009
ISBN: 978-9937-8244-4-6

Janson typeface with diacritical marks and
Tibetan Classic typeface
Designed and created by Tony Duff
Tibetan Computer Company
http://www.tibet.dk/tcc

Produced, Printed, and Published by
Padma Karpo Translation Committee
P.O. Box 4957
Kathmandu
NEPAL

Web-site and e-mail contact through:
http://www.tibet.dk/pktc
or search Padma Karpo Translation Committee on the web.

CONTENTS

INTRODUCTION

Nyingthig is a name for the innermost teaching of Great Completion. Of the various Nyingthig teachings that appeared in Tibet, Longchen Nyingthig is the Nyingthig coming from Longchen Rabjam. The Longchen Nyingthig teachings were received from Longchen Rabjam by Jigmey Lingpa in a series of visions. Jigmey Lingpa had a few very close disciples. One of them, Jigmey Trinley Ozer, became the source of a line of emanations called the Dodrupchens. The third Dodrupchen, Tenpa'i Nyima, was well-known for his teachings and writings supporting this Longchen Nyingthig system. The text here is a record of an important teaching of his on the system, found in the Dzogchen section of his *Collected Works*.

One of the important teachings of the innermost level of Great Completion, that is Nyingthig, comes from the first human holder of the teachings in this world, Garab Dorje. He gave a particular teaching to his main disciple Manjushrimitra called "The Three Lines that Strike the Key Points". The practice of the innermost level of Great Completion is summed up in two practices, one called Thorough Cut and one called Direct Crossing. The Three Lines teaching by Garab Dorje is a teaching about Thorough Cut and not about Direct Crossing.

The Three Lines teaching has been commented on by many masters of the lineage, though one of the most famous commentaries to it these days is the one by Patrul Rinpoche, who lived around the same time as Dodrupchen Tenpa'i Nyima. The actual title of Patrul Rinpoche's text is "The Feature of the Expert Glorious King" but it is often called "The Three Lines that Strike the Key Points" because of the teaching contained in it.

The colophon attached to the text here was written by someone unknown who heard a teaching on the Three Lines from the young Tenpa'i Nyima. This person says that he took notes on it when it was taught then later had it printed by woodblock. The publication was later included in the *Collected Works* of the third Dodrupchen. The person makes the interesting comment that he was aware that the content and style of his guru's explanation of the Three Lines teaching was not like the traditional, "official" way of explaining the Three Lines. He adds that he was aware that the teaching did not fit with an explanation of the Three Lines that would be found in one of the texts of the lineage that was regarded as an "authentic" teaching of the Three Lines. These are disclaimers to the effect that, even though the teaching does not fit with what a reader might expect, it does not matter because these are genuine teachings on the matter from one of the main lineage holders of the Longchen Nyingthig teaching. With that in mind, the person went ahead and cleaned up his notes and had them committed to wood blocks.

Both points were true then and true now. Tenpa'i Nyima's Three Lines teaching does not follow the traditional explanation of the Three Lines that Strike the Key points as given orally or in written down in texts that are accepted as authentic statements of the lineage. However, if you know the subject, you will see that the treatment of it is masterful and does follow the meaning of the Three Lines. In fact, the three main headings in the text are the Three Lines themselves as given by Garab Dorje. Tenpa'i Nyima himself says early in his teaching that the order is not the usual one and some details of the traditional explanation might have been left out but the entire meaning of the Three Lines teaching is there. For those familiar with the Three Lines teaching, that will be seen to be true.

One of the really interesting things about this teaching is the way that Tenpa'i Nyima includes a teaching on Direct Crossing, too. Remember that the Three Lines is a teaching for the practice of Thorough Cut. Sometimes Thorough Cut teachings include some additional comments, made in passing, about Direct Crossing. However, Tenpa'i Nyima goes further. He gives a presentation of Direct Crossing and moreover does so by weaving it in with the Thorough Cut teaching so that the whole path of innermost Great Completion is clearly shown. The teaching as given by the young Dodrupchen really is a masterful presentation.

Note that it would be very interesting for those studying Thorough Cut to read Patrul Rinpoche's perfectly traditional explanation of the Three Lines in his text that is regarded as an authentic text of the teaching. The text is *The Feature of the Expert, Glorious King* as mentioned before. A translation of Patrul Rinpoche's text and commentary is available from us; see our web-site at the address shown on the copyright page of this book. If you look at the arrangement and content of his explanation and compare it to what is here, you will understand the compiler's comments and will understand what he was thinking when he made his disclaimers. You will also find that Patrul Rinpoche's text will help you to see more clearly how parts of Tenpa'i Nyima's explanation fit into the subjects he is explaining, especially in the explanation of the second of the Three Lines. Conversely, Tenpa'i Nyima's explanations function again and again as ornaments to the traditional explanation as found in Patrul Rinpoche's text. Anyone who uses the Three Lines teaching will have many points of that teaching clarified, no doubt.

All in all, Tenpa'i Nyima's teaching makes many excellent points about both Thorough Cut and Direct Crossing practices. However, it goes a step further and mentions many points about how the two function together and also how their overall path of innermost Great Completion compares to other paths both of sutra and tantra. The text is very encompassing and should be very helpful to anyone following Thorough Cut and Direct Crossing.

Our Supports for Study

I have been encouraged over the years by all of my teachers and gurus to pass on some of the knowledge I have accumu-

The principal lineage teachers of innermost Great Completion as it came into Tibet including Garab Dorje, the source of the teaching in general and the Three Lines teaching in particular. Garab Dorje above left, Manjushrimitra above right, Vimalamitra below left, Shri Singha below right of Padmasambhava in the centre. Mural on the wall of Dzogchen Monastery, Tibet, 2007. Photograph by the author.

lated in a lifetime dedicated to the study and practice, primarily through the Tibetan Buddhist tradition, of Buddhism. On the one hand they have encouraged me to teach. On the other hand, they are concerned that, while many general books on Buddhism have been and are being published, there are few books that present the actual texts of the tradition. They and many other, closely involved people have encouraged me to make and publish high quality translations of individual texts of the tradition.

In general, we have published a wide range of books that present the important literature of Tibetan Buddhism. In particular, the author of this book was one of the very important figures in the transmission of the most profound Great Completion teachings in Tibet and we have published many of the important texts of that system, with each one carefully selected to inform about a particular aspect of that teaching. We produced this book because it presents the same teaching of Thorough Cut as the very famous *Feature of the Expert Glorious King* by Patrul Rinpoche but does it in a completely different way. The two texts are so complementary that, in my opinion, if you are going to read one, you should read the other. In addition to Patrul's text, we also recommend these publications of ours that concern the practice of Thorough Cut as supports for this book: *Alchemy of Accomplishment* by Dudjom Jigdral Yeshe Dorje; *Essential Points of Practice* by Zhechen Gyaltshab; *Way of the Old Dogs* by Ju Mipham Namgyal; *Hinting at Dzogchen* by Tony Duff; *Peak Doorways to Emancipation* by Shakya Shri; and other titles which are being added all the time.

Another of the features of this text is that it also present Direct Crossing. As supports for that part of the teaching, there is our publication of *Key Points of Direct Crossing called Nectar of the Pure Part* by Khenchen Padma Namgyal. Also, the author has prepared Jigmey Lingpa's most important text *Wisdom Guru, a Guidebook to the Stages of the Path of the Primordial Guardian According to Longchen Nyingthig Great Completion* which contains a very extensive presentation of Direct Crossing. It should be noted that this translation is quite different from the one published by Snow Lion in which there are many mistakes and pieces of the text are missing; this translation is complete, accurate, and with hundreds of detailed notes. Both of these are restricted publications.

All in all, you will find many books both for free and for sale on our web-site, all of them prepared to the highest level of quality. Many of our books are available not only on paper but as electronic editions that can be downloaded, and all of them are prepared to the highest level of quality. We encourage you to look at our web-site to see what we have; the address is on the copyright page at the front of this book. Major book sellers also carry our paper editions.

It has also been a project of ours to make tools that non-Tibetans and Tibetans alike could use for the study and translation of Tibetan texts. As part of that project, we prepare electronic editions of Tibetan texts in the Tibetan Text input office of the Padma Karpo Translation Committee and make them available to the world. Tibetan texts are often corrupt so we make a special point of carefully correcting our work before making it available through our web-site. Thus, our electronic texts are not careless productions like most Tibetan texts found on the web but are highly reliable editions that can be used by non-scholars and scholars alike. Moreover, many of the texts are free. The Tibetan text for this book is available for download as a free, electronic edition. It is also included at the back of the book as an aid to serious study.

Our electronic texts can be read, searched, and so on, using our Tibetan software. The software can be used to set up a reference library of these texts and then used to read and even research them quickly and easily. The software, called TibetD and TibetDoc, has many special features that make it useful not only for reading but also for understanding and even translating texts. One key feature is that you can highlight a Tibetan term in a text then look it up immediately in any of our electronic dictionaries. We suggest the highly acclaimed *Illuminator Tibetan-English Dictionary* as the best dictionary for the purpose. As with all of our publications, the software and electronic texts can be obtained from our web-site whose address is on the copyright page at the front of the book.

Health Warning

The text here is about a subject that is kept secret. Therefore, I have translated the text as it is, providing enough notes so that someone who does understand the meaning could understand the translation without mistake. However, I have deliberately not given any further explanation of or commentary to the meaning. Anyone who has had these teachings in person will be able to understand them or at least go to his teacher and ask for further explanation. Anyone who has heard these teachings in person from a qualified teacher, and especially who has had the introduction to the nature of mind[1] around which the teachings hinge, please use and enjoy the texts as you will! However, if you have not heard these teachings and if you have not had a proper introduction to the nature of your mind, you would be better off not reading this book but seeking out someone who could teach it to you. These days there are both non-Tibetans and Tibetans who can do that for you and who are available in many countries across our planet. In short, the contents of this book could be dangerous to your spiritual health if you are not ready for it, so exercise care.

These days, in the times of rampant globalization, these deep secrets have become very public. That is not necessarily a good thing. For example, I have many times in the last few years run into young men who are extremely confident of their understanding of the meaning of these profound systems but who just spout words that they have read in books. Unfortunately, they have read the books and know the words but have not contacted the inner meaning that the books are intended to be merely a pointer towards. The solidity of their minds is noticeable and it is not being helped by reading these things that they are not ready for and should not be reading.

With endless prostrations
To the Dodrupchen beings

---

[1] Introduction to the nature of mind is mostly mis-translated these days as "pointing out" instruction.

And a constant stream of
Thanks to all of them …

PHAT cuts the elaboration,
HUM HUM HUM is the song of the dharmakaya arrived at,
PHEM PHEM PHEM is the warmth of the empty space,
HO HO HO is father christmas giving you the goods.

Lama Tony Duff,
Swayambhunath,
Nepal,
February 2009

ABOUT THE THREE LINES THAT STRIKE THE KEY POINTS by Dodrupchen III Tenpa'i Nyima

I prostrate with great respect at the feet of the guru who wholly embodies the Three Supremes[2].

Here in regard to this[3], there are two styles of path meditation that, based on the force of experience, make luminosity manifest. Of them, the style of the other sections of unsurpassed tantra[4] in which it is manifested through working the key points in the channels, drops, and winds, is as follows. It does not require that the aspect of luminosity be explained at

---

[2] The Three Supremes is a name for the Three Jewels.

[3] These words are the standard Tibetan way of indicating that the main part of a lecture or text has just been commenced now that the prefatory remarks or materials have been done with.

[4] Great Completion is one of the three sections of unsurpassed tantra. The three are: Mahayoga, Anuyoga, and Atiyoga, with the latter being another name for Great Completion. Here he is referring to Mahayoga and Anuyoga.

first[5] rather, the luminosity is made to shine forth when the key points of the channel chakras of the heart or navel, and so on are worked. When that luminosity does shine forth, for the special kind of person for whom all appearing objects then shine forth as great bliss, that luminosity of equipoise will also be brought forth as luminosity in post-attainment just by the force of that person deliberately remembering it. The reason for that is exemplified by a mother whose only son dies. She will be so stricken with grief that, even if she goes to pleasing places like garden groves, it will not make her happy; no matter where she goes, she will never find happiness there, only suffering. Similarly, if a person who craves wealth finds a wish-fulfilling jewel in his hand, his mind will become so saturated with joy that, even if he is boxed up into a very tight place, he will never become unhappy, and will stay only joyful. In the same way, acquaintance with great-bliss wisdom at the time of equipoise makes it possible later on at the time of post-attainment, to bring the great-bliss wisdom forth without needing to work the key points of channels, drops, and winds, just by remembering it.

In the path of Great Completion, it is not necessary to have that extra meditation on channels, drops, and winds. Instead, at first, based on the guru's foremost instructions[6], you

---

[5] Innermost Great Completion does require that luminosity be explained right at the beginning.

[6] Tib. man ngag. Foremost instructions are a special type of instruction. See the glossary for more. Innermost Great Completion depends on foremost instructions above all.

continuously attend to a mindfulness that uninterruptedly minds rigpa[7], which is the way to preserve[8] rigpa.

Those foremost instructions of the guru are to the point that this luminosity of death and becoming is like a ground where all of this life's appearance-mind is contained and where all later lives' appearances will be ignited. That exactly is the luminosity that is everywhere empty or, you can say, the primordially liberated, uncompounded rigpa. That, the final, subtle awareness from which all appearances ignite, is called "rigpa" or "luminosity". Primordially, that luminosity has never experienced being existent. Suddenly popping up mind has never occurred in the character of that rigpa. "Suddenly popping up mind" as it is called is those suddenly born awarenesses that are the sense faculty consciousnesses and, more subtle than that, the mind consciousness. The fact of the luminosity is such that primordially, from the outset, its character has been untainted by this sudden popping up, therefore it is called "alpha purity". If we take the alphabet, literally meaning "the letter A and all the ones beyond it included", then substitute "alpha purity", we get in a similar way the "alpha" purity and beyond that, the entire contents of

---

[7] Rigpa is not translated in this text because there are no English words that are sufficient. See the glossary for an explanation.

[8] To preserve or, you could say, "maintain", is a key term of Great Completion vocabulary. It refers to the way that a desired state is not cultivated but is simply preserved. The difference is that cultivation, also called meditation, is a technique for creating something new that was not there before. Preservation on the other hands, simply preserves, in the current moment, a direct perception of what is already there.

Great Completion's path included with it. This is connected with the key point of "alpha purity", "the outset", "the beginning"[9], and so on having the same meaning.

Furthermore, the luminosity has the evenness of being free of the ups and downs of agitation that come from thought proliferation and sinking-dullness but, because the winds, and so on, on which the sensory and mental consciousnesses ride, are not present in its character, it never accumulates any of what would be the mind side, so it has transparency[10]. Being like a butter lamp inside a vase, the internalized luminosity or deep luminosity is called "the youthful vase body". That rigpa has an intensity of luminosity greater than that of one hundred suns, therefore it is "self-illuminating"[11]. The three of bliss, clarity, and no-thought are inherently present in it[12], therefore it is "spontaneous existence"[13]. The mind of the first dhyana is more subtle than that of the desire realm, that of the second is more subtle than that of the first, and so on; the nature of this is that the ones below are more subtle than the ones above and this awareness, being even more subtle than any of those, is exceedingly subtle.

---

[9] The Tibetan for these three words is "ka dag", "gdod ma", and "thog ma" respectively.

[10] See the glossary.

[11] Tib. rang gsal.

[12] They are inherently in it because non-thought is the essence, empty; clarity is the nature, luminosity; and bliss is the two of them functioning as all-pervasive compassionate activity.

[13] Tib. lhun grub.

All of the above items draw out and show one by one the various features of rigpa, this is done because of the need to gain an intellectual understanding of its features. To gain an understanding of rigpa's way of being seated that is based in its own way of understanding requires being introduced to it. To digest it raw requires full comprehension of it which is achieved through preserving it with mindfulness.[14]

For you to be introduced through the guru's foremost instructions to luminosity's way of being seated requires being able to be acquainted with it on the face of mental mind, without having discarded mind and left it behind. If you were to discard it, that would be to destroy the life of the path of Thorough Cut. It would be equivalent, for example, to positing for the other unsurpassed tantra sections that there is no need to work the key points of channels, drops, and so on, and thereby destroying the life of completion stage. Mind, which can be separated out into pure and impure parts, is the impure part, and rigpa is the quintessential, highly-refined, pure portion wrapped up in it.

---

[14] This is a threefold journey. First you are introduced to it in words and gain an intellectual understanding of its qualities. Next you are introduced to it as an actual experience that comes from a way of knowing that is its own way of knowing; this is called "introduction" (see the glossary for more about introduction). Finally, if you want to be in direct contact with it unmodified so that you just have the whole thing as it is, called "digesting it raw", you have to realize it fully, which is also called "fully comprehending it", and that is done by continuous practice of it, which is characterized as the practice of "preserving".

With the latencies of not-rigpa[15] exhausted, the thing that accomplishes buddhahood is rigpa. Having made rigpa into the path and preserved it by a mindfulness that never disconnects from it for even a moment, if it is there with rational mind having been made enormously vast, then the possibility of digesting the rigpa raw will have been discovered and, when that happens, there will have been an introduction to rigpa[16]. In raw rigpa, the suddenly popping up mind *per se* cannot arise and the actuality[17] is changeless therefore it has to be understood as "unaltered", "dharmakāya rigpa", and "the basis of the accomplishment of dharmakāya".

The name "rigpa" in Great Completion is a designation of a convention; it is called[18] "rigpa" because it is an awareness beyond the three appearances which is the basis for the accom-

---

[15] Tib. ma rig pa. Usually translated as "ignorance" but that is a non-literal translation that totally breaks the reader's comprehension of the play between the two states of rigpa and not-rigpa, which is actually the whole story of samsara and nirvana.

[16] There is a point here. Rational mind is usually regarded as a bogeyman in these discussions because it is the epitome of dualistic mind. However, if you can build an enormous vastness with lack of clinging, then it is possible to have a mind that discriminates this and that but which is not dualistic. At that point, you can eat raw rigpa. The first time that you do that, you have the introduction.

[17] The fundamental reality of the ground state which has now been met ...

[18] By the former ones of the lineage.

plishment of dharmakāya[19] and it is called "luminosity" because that rigpa has never experienced shrouding by darkness. What in mother tantra is called "great bliss co-emergent wisdom" refers to great bliss and co-emergence where a separation into two primordially has never been experienced so, existing as a co-emergence, it is called "co-emergent wisdom"; it is the luminosity that is the ground where all of this life's appearance-mind is contained and where all later lives' appearances will be ignited. When the luminosity is being governed by total conceptuality[20] and mind[21], there is

---

[19] Rigpa, meaning to have dynamic, direct knowledge, is a type of awareness. Therefore, the thing that the name is to be applied to would also have to be an awareness. It is, but it is not just any awareness, it is one that is beyond the appearances of the three realms of samsara. Moreover, this awareness is the very thing that you practise in order to attain the dharmakāya. It is a dynamic knowledge of an enlightened type.

[20] Tib. kun rtog. This is the surface-most layer of the ignorance of a sentient being. The mind stays within a process of only thinking conceptually which is a type of ignorance in itself but is also a defence mechanism that prevents the more basic levels of ignorance from self-collapse.

[21] Tib. sems. Tibetan texts distinguish all types of mind clearly so that when they are being discussed the listener knows exactly what is being discussed. Our translations always follow this approach. Here and throughout this text, "mind" by itself nearly always refers to samsaric mind. (The only time it does not is one occasion where a term for mind that normally means samsaric mind is used to mean all types of mind, both enlightened and unenlightened.) This is a key point for understanding the text

(continued...)

no knowing where it will go which fits with its being called "primordially liberated, uncompounded"[22].

I. Introduction to Oneself

The way in which there is "introduction to oneself[23]" is as follows. "To oneself" means introduction to the luminosity itself. The way of doing the introduction is, as stated above, that the guru's foremost instructions show the fact of the luminosity or the luminosity's way of being seated, just exactly as it is. An understanding happens for the disciple because of the introduction which then has to be made into a certainty.

An example for the way of doing the introduction is this. When the sky is obscured by thick clouds, any attempt to introduce the sky will meet with some difficulty. If some parts of the sky are free of cloud, then, a little bit of the sky being visible, an introduction to it can be made by saying, "All of this world's sky is blue like this", and it will be easy for the introduction to occur. Like that, in the situation now of

---

[21](...continued)
according to what the author intended.

[22] If samsaric mind takes it over, because samsaric mind has infinite possibilities, it can and does go anywhere in the unenlightened side, that points at the fact that the luminosity itself is an uncompounded, meaning not created by karma and not subject to cause and effect, thing. It has been and always will be, so it is primordially liberated.

[23] The first of the Three Lines.

massed clouds of total conceptuality and the various strands of mind, any attempt to introduce luminosity will meet with some difficulty. However, if the luminosity that shines forth at the times of death and dharmatā bardos is introduced in this same situation, the introduction will occur; for it, the guru tells the disciple in detail how the luminosity shines forth at the times of death and dharmatā bardos then the disciple must, based on his own understanding obtained according to that explanation, arrive at a very detailed experience of it. Those various points comprise "introduction to oneself".

2. Decision on One Thing

That luminosity exists in the cave of your own present awareness[24] as something that you never are separated from for even a moment, in the same way as a sesame seed is permeated by oil; if you did separate from it, neither buddhas nor sentient beings would be supported[25]. Now, you must come to the point of deciding on one thing, which is that you do have it as such. You might think, "Even though it is present in me like that, this luminosity will shine forth at death but, other than that, will not shine forth in me now, will it?", but

---

[24] This is a Tibetan way of talking. Here, cave has the sense of "that (special) place within" and has a sense of endearment with it.

[25] If you could separate from it, then the only two possibilities of your continuing existence, that of a buddha or a sentient being, would cease to be. That is not possible, so you are never separated from this fundamental luminosity.

that is not correct—it shines forth at the times of death, fainting, and so on[26].

You do not plant that luminosity in the present moment the way that it was done for you when you were introduced to it, a time when it was parted from something to be mindful of and something that stays mindful of it[27]. Instead, and similar to a person remembering himself by himself, first you have to use mindfulness to put everything of mind's side as non significant, un-necessary, and then, having made rigpa's side alone shine forth on the face of mind you have to meditate in an uncontrived way on rigpa's nature. If, through mindfulness, you discard that fact of rigpa, then you will bring forth something based in mind[28]. For example, if you fall off a bed

---

[26] There is a teaching on the particular circumstances in which it does shine forth. The "and so on" indicates the rest of the items mentioned in that list and is effectively inserting that teaching at this point. One of the items in the list includes its shining forth through the special techniques of introduction and the possibility of practising it after that. That then leads on to the next paragraph's content ...

[27] He is saying, now that you have been introduced, you have to get on with the actual practice of it. That usually does not happen, though it could, with you just jumping straight into the full experience, like it was shown to you at the introduction which has the particular quality of being beyond dualistic types of mindfulness. Instead, you start with the dualistic mindfulness and work from there. This is a slightly path oriented way of explaining how to do the practice and it does end up being true for most people.

[28] Here he means, if you impose a dualistic kind of mindfulness,

(continued...)

in a house, you don't leave the house, and similar to this example, if that rigpa gets discarded through mindfulness, you end up still not leaving mind[29].

If you meditate in clear and highly alert mind, that will not fulfill the needs of rigpa meditation. This can be illustrated as follows. "Fourth part free of three", meaning the fourth part free of the three parts, can be called rigpa. The reason is that, because of the key point that one part of mind is rigpa, designating it as "rigpa" is all right. If rigpa is introduced at the time of the fourth part free from the three, the introduction will go easily. In that case, it will be like a sketch done in artist's colours.[30]

When the preserving of rigpa by mindfulness has been undertaken, it is not necessary to think, "Is the manifestation of rigpa happening?" To set up an example, when there is a row of people in a room and all eyes are on one of them, the rest of the people become not thought of at all but they have not gradually dissolved into that one man nor are they sitting there being watched with one corner of the mind. Similar to

---

[28](...continued)
like you did in the first step, that will cause the rigpa to be lost and a return to mind, which is not what you want.

[29] Again dualistic mind.

[30] This is making a point about a way to do the introduction. The teaching on four parts free from three must be obtained in person. An introduction done in those circumstances will be a particular good one in which everything is seen clearly and with an economy of extra movement, so to speak.

them not being thought of at all, when you are meditating by looking at rigpa with mindfulness, a sort of merging of the mindfulness with rigpa does occur. There is no need to be taking interest[31] in that, thinking, "Have they merged?" And, in the present moment there is no need either to be thinking about whether the luminosity shining forth has happened. For example, when you meditate on a buddha adorned with the major marks and the form of the buddha is there, appearing in your mind, it is not necessary to be thinking about it with, "My meditation on buddha is happening", because the buddha meditation is already happening in your mind. Similarly, it is not necessary to be thinking about this with, "There is luminosity shining forth for me" because the luminosity that the guru introduced you to previously is what you are right now in the process of meditating on! Orgyan Rinpoche said,

> "Outwardly-directed grasping, and so on sorts of things are dealt with in luminosity self-recognizing itself …"

meaning that, for as long as you are preserving rigpa using mindfulness of the rigpa that was introduced through the guru's foremost instructions, the luminosity is recognizing itself and, due to that, the appearing objects of the outwardly-

---

[31] Interest is one of the many mental events, described, for example, in the fifty-two mental events. Thus, it has a two-fold meaning here. The main point is that pursuit of the issue is not necessary. There is an implied understanding which is that this kind of interest is necessarily a resumption of dualistic mind and that, by its mere presence, will have already caused the rigpa to have been discarded.

directed grasping proceed to purification of themselves[32]. When you stay there meditating on the basis of having mixed mindfulness and rigpa, then the mind of the inwardly-directed grasper will dissolve into the rigpa or, you can say, naturally proceed to being pure. Similarly, for as long as you stay there preserving rigpa using mindfulness not to forget it, there is the certainty that doing so will proceed as luminosity recognizing itself. When you have worked at preserving that rigpa, then, like water goes where it is already wet, minds[33]

---

[32] Here and elsewhere in the text, you will find the pair of terms grasped-grasping. This is a mind-only way of talking that is used throughout the higher tantras. One aspect of mind is the external objects that are being grasped at and the other aspect is the internal grasper, the subject, that is knowing the grasped at object. One moment of mind with both facets is the point. They are both mind so there is no actual external or internal object or subject but the deluded, samsaric mind believes that the externally directed grasped at aspect is an external item and that the internally directed grasping aspect is an internal item. Both are wrong and collapse in the face of rigpa, which solves in one stroke the whole problem of samsara. Tenpa'i Nyima defines Thorough Cut in another text as "the direct severance of grasped-grasping" which is the meaning of all of this.

[33] This does not merely mean that "thoughts" will be elaborated from the rigpa. It means that whole minds with perceived object and perceiving subject to them will be elaborated. In this case though, you are not falling into a dualized not-rigpa (ignorance) type of mind but are keeping the apparent duality within non-dualistic rigpa. We have moved past the beginner's stage here and are talking about how you can have, for example, an apparently normal human existence with known objects and a knowing

(continued...)

will be elaborated from the liveliness of the rigpa because of which, in the end, the minds do appear but proceed through dissolving back into the rigpa itself; in other words, the rigpa can and will find the path that belongs to its own way of being. For example, just as waves that come from the ocean do in the end dissolve back into it, the minds that are the liveliness of the rigpa are elaborated from the rigpa and, in the end, due to the force of path meditation, the liveliness proceeds to dissolve back into the rigpa itself or to become pure in rigpa's expanse so, at that time, it is called, "a mind of movement that self-purifies[34]".

---

[33](...continued)
subject, just like everyone else, but with the key difference that, although there is an observed polarity, there is no grasped duality. The way of saying that according to the tradition is that "the minds that are elaborated are not the liveliness of not-rigpa (ignorance) but of rigpa" and he mentions this just below. This is a very profound part of the teaching and can be easily misunderstood. "Minds" here connects with the fruition state of an enlightened kind of "mind" which is mentioned in footnote 34.

[34] Here the word for mind is the honorific form, which is only used to mean a mind that is beyond samsaric dualistic mind. It is the same word as mind but its honorific form indicates a different type of operation. Instead of spewing out concepts that only serve to solidify the dualistic mind that has produced them, this mind makes all the same stuff as the dualistic mind but all of it goes on to self-purity because of being included within the realm of the luminosity. This last, long paragraph contains a whole progression of practice, from the beginner's level of making a decision on one thing to someone who has become very adept at doing so. In other words, it goes from someone who has just

(continued...)

The restraint of the sense faculties' doors is, in development stage, in post attainment, that the container and contents are viewed as the universal purity, the deity mandala, and in completion stage, that which appears is viewed as a great bliss play, and in this case here, that the liveliness has been trained up so that what appears comes as a crystal clear bliss[35] in the rigpa's liveliness or in the rigpa's gadgetry[36].[37]

---

[34](...continued)
been introduced to rigpa for the first time up to someone who is becoming adept at being in rigpa with everything entailed by it. There is more to go though.

[35] Crystal clear bliss means a bliss that is within an environment where all the stuff of dualistic mind has been cleared out so that only the pure portion, which in this teaching of nyingthig is rigpa, remains.

[36] Rigpa's gadgetry means the stuff made up by rigpa and brought into manifestation. It's rigpa's stuff, the things it invents and uses in its operation.

[37] This is pointing at the fruition level of the practice. The restraint of the sense faculty doors means making a proper relationship to the external phenomena that appear to the senses. Every level of Buddhist practice has its own way of talking about what this means. Here he gives two. He mentions the approach of the other unsurpassed tantras in their development and completion stages, then he mentions the approach of this innermost Great Completion. In Great Completion, the special language for this is "to train up the liveliness" which refers to the whole path after rigpa has been introduced and recognized up to the final conclusion. When one has reached the end of the training, one is not merely dealing with the emptiness of the rigpa or with its mental

(continued...)

In short, mind and rigpa are distinguished as that to be rejected and to be adopted respectively. Having done so, rigpa's way of being seated must be preserved by mindfulness. That sort of preservation moreover, first has to be done in meditation that uses a conceptual-effort type of mindfulness to mix with the rigpa, whereas at the end, formative-type mindfulnesses[38] will have become self-purifying, so will shine forth internal to the rigpa as part of its own complexion[39] and at that time are called, "mindfulness without conceptual efforts that is self-placed".

It is said again and again, with great insistence that, "Once that primordially liberated, uncompounded rigpa existing as its own awareness has been introduced through the guru's foremost instructions, a decision about it definitely must be made". Doing this here, like there, is not thought of as a fault but is done while listing the main points to be remembered according to the order of the topics in the explanation.

---

[37](...continued)
manifestations but is now capable of allowing it in full manifestation of the senses, as well.

[38] Formatives are the content of the fourth skandha. They receive their name because they are specifically what cause the formation of future sets of skandhas in future beings. In other words, they drive the process of becoming in samsara. Any kind of conceptual mindfulness will be like that. The point is that the path includes getting beyond those kind of samsara-forming mindfulnesses to ones that are part of the rigpa itself.

[39] For complexion of rigpa see the glossary. The image is one of not being the empty portion but the lustre that appears on it.

The luminosity rigpa like that is luminosity rigpa as it is determined by the Great Completion lineage. The lineage has taught many ways to determine it, such as with the twelve vajra laughters, the eight great words, the seven types of resting methods, the four types of Chog Zhag, and so on. It is being taught here using the key points of the Three Lines and, even though the explanation here does not include all the wording connected with that, it does include all of the meaning.

From among the twelve vajra laughters, the meaning expressed in, "Great Completion is the dharma that transcends cause and effect HA HA" is not a denigration of the cause and effect of other vehicles but relates to the fact that both cause and effect exist on top of mind that starts up from the three appearances[40]. It is said that for those who go to the character of Great Completion, for both those who committed the five immediates[41] and those who accumulated the accumulations during many kalpas there is no difference in their going to buddhahood; this statement is made from the perspective of their minding[42] primordially liberated, uncompounded rigpa. (Note in text itself: this is a teaching using Great Completion's own way of talking that accords with what the words

---

[40] The appearances of the three realms of samsara.

[41] The five immediates are five of the heaviest karmic actions. They are so heavy that, when the person dies, there is immediate birth in hell without intermediary bardo. Hence the name.

[42] As in an earlier note, this is the honorific for the usual mind and implies full realization.

lead to[43], namely, "not contaminated by virtue or evil"; there is no explanation or teaching of such a thing for those who have not gone to that character). This would be for yogins like Telopa and Vimala who have gone to the character denoted by the name[44]. "Samantabhadra even was buddha without having made the slightest virtue and without having abandoned the slightest evil" is speaking beyond virtue and evil and also is speaking of minding[45] the single, unique sphere of luminosity. The reason for it is that, because the luminosity has never experienced contamination by any of the sufferings of fire of the hot hells, cold of the cold hells, hunger and thirst of the pretas, and so on, the luminosity cannot arise as the entity of suffering; thus it is being stated according to what the words lead to. In sum, it is a very important point that it does posit the experiencing of result in relation to having accumulated causes on top of the coarse appearance-mind that operates prior to the three of appearance, flaring, and attainment, and so on[46]. As was said,

---

[43] Not what the words mean literally.

[44] Great Completion's character.

[45] Honorific again.

[46] Appearance, flaring, and attainment are the last three stages of the death process. He is saying that there are results that will come from causes created in this life, that is, up to the very end of this life at the end of the death process when this life's mind dissolves. The "and so on" does not go with "appearance, flaring, and attainment" but means "and all the other ways that causes are accumulated. Why does he say that? Because "coarse appearance-mind" refers to the mind of the desire realm. Karmic causes

(continued...)

> "Samantabhadra, not having done even a speck of virtue,
> By the accumulation of virtue belonging to self-recognition of the un-outflowed[47] ..."

Compared to abandoning external entertainments and practising for one hundred years, it is more profitable to stay alone in an isolated mountain tract for one day practising virtue and in that case your own mind being very clean and pure is that external, isolation of a mountain tract. Internally, isolation from discursive thoughts is that, generally, having practised the shamatha-vipashyana of the paramita vehicles and having because of it a body and mind that have been made serviceable so that one has the control to be able to put mind and have it stay or send it and have it go, whatever it references will serve only to pull one off[48] into virtue. The sky-like luminosity in which the strands of discursive thought have been cut is set down as the secret level mountain tract;

---

[46](...continued)
are also accumulated in the lives of beings in the form and formless realm and they do inevitably lead to results, too. Thus the "and so on" refers to the all the other possibilities of karmic cause creation that lead to results.

This point here is that Great Completion does not leave out the teaching of karmic cause and effect even though the attainment of its fruition might seem at times to bypass it. This follows on from the discussion just a little earlier.

[47] See glossary.

[48] Which is a sense of isolation ...

in relation to the luminosity, the fact of the mastery of being able to put mind and have it stay and send it and have it go is also said to be a shroud of pollution, so the secret one is the mountain tract isolated from mind.[49]

Then, there is the rate of travel of this path. The path of the Paramita Vehicle possessing both profound and vast aspects practised for many uncountable kalpas finally leads to manifest buddhahood. The mantra path is extremely quick compared to that; the paths of the three, outer tantra sections accomplish the ordinary siddhis, and so on then, after lives extending through many kalpas, the supreme siddhi is at last attained. On the path of the other unsurpassed tantra sections, the supreme siddhi can be obtained without having to extend it into other lives, in twelve human years. This path at the very peak of the nine vehicles attains the supreme siddhi in six human years. Such are the differing rates of travel.

In short, the alpha purity Thorough Cut's rigpa way of being situated within the context of the luminosity of death and

---

[49] Here, he has given the standard definitions of outer, inner, secret, and innermost retreats. The outer retreat is to stay in an isolated mountain place (or other place depending on the country involved). Doing that is much more virtuous than staying in town and doing virtuous things. Staying in the mountains is equivalent to purifying your motivation and turning your mind to the dharma. So, in fact, if you do purify your motivation and turn your mind to the dharma properly, then you have the outer retreat, no matter where you are. And then it goes on from there …

becoming is introduced just as it is. Then, each of its various qualities are shown via the various ways of expressing its features such as alpha purity, transparency[50], and so on. Then, rigpa's way of being situated is introduced well through the guru's foremost instructions and, having done so, it is then, in one's own mindfulness of the present, to be well and definitely acquainted with. This sort of rigpa does not exist as a fact in some place other than that; one makes a decision that this, one's own awareness of the present just now explained, is it. Then, based on having made that decision, one does not do an interest-type meditation[51] with a thought like, "With mindfulness not having forgotten the fact of that rigpa for even a moment, this mind of mine has become the entity of rigpa", rather, all of these factors of one's own awareness of the present are to be viewed as being the nature of rigpa and, not wavering in the slightest to the mind side, rigpa's side is to be meditated on well, and that is the uncommon key point of meaning. That completes "decision on one thing".

3. Assurance Built on Liberation

Of the three types of meditation, best, middling, and least, the best meditation is like throwing a stone at a lion. When a stone is thrown at a lion, the lion is not driven off but turns on the stone thrower and the retaliation means that the stone will not be thrown again. Similarly, the best meditation does not follow after discursive thought when it suddenly erupts but causes the agent behind the shining forth of the discursive

---

[50] See the glossary.

[51] Per previous note, interest implies samsaric mind.

thought to remember himself so that he apprehends himself all of a sudden and then, whatever discursive thoughts arise, they are sent on into self-liberation. The meaning of what some say about this, "Look directly at the discursive thought", is that the discursive thought looks at itself. What some say, "Look in between the previous and next discursive thought at the mind clear and vivid", also has that same meaning. Those two do not matter; instead there is the meaning of, "Look directly at how it is", which is for rigpa to look at itself. This case of looking at rigpa and its not causing even the slightest self because of mindfulness on mind's side is the single meaning of the key points of this context. The least meditation is like a stone thrown at a dog, with the stone causing the dog to leave the thrower and be driven off by the stone. Similarly the agent behind the shining forth of the discursive thought is left behind but it is not that the meditation goes off, driven away by the discursive thought, instead it looks at the agent of the shining forth, himself[52].

There are three ways of liberation. "Recognizing discursive thought like meeting a man you know from before" is that, if the fact of the rigpa is forgotten, what happens is that a discursive thought that shines forth will be recognized as such and then, having seen it as a fault, you put yourself back on rigpa's way of being situated as it was before.

---

[52] When discursive thought shines forth, the meditation forgets about the agent that causes it like the dog leaves the stone-thrower behind. Unlike in the example, the meditation does not head away in the direction of the discursive thought like the dog heads off in the direction of the thrown stone, instead, it sits looks right at the thrower of the stone.

"Discursive thought self-liberating itself" is the way of liberation like that of knots in a snake collapsing. At the time the fact of rigpa's way of being seated is made into the path, another discursive thought is not able to cause an interruption. However, mindfulness has slightly tightened the rigpa so there is danger of distraction if the rigpa does not get preserved. Thus, a slight force of tightening makes the discursive thought unable to plant itself and it is liberated in its own place.

Third, the way of "discursive thought being liberated without benefit, without harm" is like if a thief comes into an empty house, there is no benefit for the thief and no harm to the materials of the house. At this time, you are already planted in the space of rigpa by mindfulness so that, even though ordinary discursive thoughts pop in, there is nothing to be gained for the discursive thought and nothing to be lost for the luminosity.

In sum, it is necessary to have that spear of mindfulness planted in the depths of rigpa so that no circumstance of something other than it[53] has the ability to wrest it away; it should not be like the flashing in and out that goes up and down a river when white powder is scattered onto water[54].

---

[53] A "circumstance" has the sense of something that could turn into a discursive thought but which is not a discursive thought yet. However, here, the circumstance never gets to ripen into its possibility.

[54] The mindfulness has to be a deep part of the rigpa, not a (continued...)

Then, step by step, the restrictive type of mindfulness or the formative-type mindfulness[55] comes to an end and a mindfulness that comes from the face of the luminosity itself is made to wake up more and more. Due to its waking, a special mindfulness that exists in the rigpa itself comes about, which is called "mindfulness without conceptual effort that is self-placed".

Training up the liveliness of the rigpa is like this[56]. The force of staying equipoised on the rigpa of equipoise causes everything at post-attainment to shine forth in the aspect of crystal clear bliss[57]. For example, like a person who sees a delightful vase, the force at the time of equipoise of not wavering from the fact of the rigpa's way of being present to another mind causes, in post-attainment, all appearing objects to shine forth

---

[54](...continued)
surface event that comes and goes.

[55] Formative-type mindfulness was discussed in a previous note. Restrictive mindfulness is a standard term of mindfulness that is trying to restrain something. This is the commonly explained type of mindfulness, for example, the one usually explained in the sutra teachings. The mindfulness needed here is the mindfulness of the dharmatā of luminosity, which is totally unrestrictive because it has no dualistic thought of something to be restricted and something to do the restricting with it.

[56] As mentioned in an earlier note, training up the liveliness is the training of rigpa that goes beyond merely accessing the empty factor and which allows the potential for the display of rigpa to become fully operative.

[57] See earlier note.

as something having an aspect of crystal clear bliss and that person for whom it shines forth like that is able to make all that appears into the gadgetry of rigpa. When that is possible, such a tantrika is able to put all the external and what is inside it, that is, containers and contents, into the gadgetry of rigpa. Thus, through the key point that all containers and contents are not existent by way of their own entity, the yogin by the force of path meditation is able to put them into rigpa's gadgetry so is able to determine both containers and contents as lacking in truth.

Furthermore, in the case of the three of initial arising, then dwelling, and going[58], it is necessary to come to a determination that mind has no ground and is free of a root. The reason for having to do this is that there is the equipoise of a meditation that makes the fact of rigpa into the path, then there is the post-attainment that comes from getting up from that, and that post-attainment is involved with undertaking the training up of the liveliness of rigpa, so it is the time for determining that appearing objects are without truth. Thus, rational mind is trained in emptiness first then, at the time of being equipoised on the liberating ground, alpha purity rigpa, there is, apart from the key point of only being in rigpa's way

---

[58] The examination of mind to see where it initially comes from, if it does come from somewhere, where it stays after that, if it does stay somewhere, and where it goes to in the end, if it does go somewhere, is one of the ways of determining that mind is groundless, rootless which is equivalent to determining its emptiness as it moves. This examination is officially included as a preliminary to Thorough Cut and Direct Crossing in the practices called "Parting into the sides of samsara and nirvana".

of being seated, also the key point of not stealing away rigpa's seat by doing analysis for emptiness, and so on.

When rigpa has been manifested, it is necessary in the context of Thorough Cut to mix expanse and rigpa. In regard to that, rigpa's entity, which is an emptiness of not existing by way of own nature, and expanse have the same meaning; that which has a nature that is an empty self-complexion whose luminosity has no stoppage in it is rigpa. If meditation is done through having mixed together both that rigpa and its expanse, emptiness, then that is expanse and rigpa having been mixed. No matter how much you familiarize yourself with emptiness using the path of Paramita Vehicle, meditation done through mixing expanse and rigpa because of this profound path is matchless in comparison. The way to understand this is that it does not happen due to there being something better or worse about the emptiness of the appearing object but because of a difference in the perceiving subject of rigpa or, you can say, the basis for the accomplishment.

The profound path of this sort practised because of seeking out one's own peace alone is said to be like making charcoal in a supreme forest of sandalwood; merely seeking what is meaningful for one's own purposes alone is not the path of the supreme vehicle, Great Completion. If, with the thought of renunciation, you do meditation only on emptiness, you will be able to obtain some kind of emancipation but just that is not enough. You need to be motivated by a mind that cannot withstand the suffering of all sentient beings even for one hour. In order to have a quick attainment of the rank of a buddha in one short life of this time of the dregs, it is necessary, having heard the oral instructions of Great Completion, to practise.

No matter what practice is attempted in either sutra or tantra, there is no difference in the two form bodies that will be accomplished but there is a difference in the path that accomplishes them. I will give a brief summary of the path presentations in a way that is appropriate to the current discussion. The path of the other unsurpassed tantras is to resort to the channels, drops, winds, and so on and, by the force of working their key points, to manifest the great-bliss wisdom like the sky free of the three circumstances that cause arousal. Having done so, wisdom accomplishes the dharmakāya. Rigpa that begins to flow out a little from that, conditions that make the luminosity co-emerge with it, and the cause of close-taking[59] of the wind's five wind lights, arise in the aspect of support and supported, a deity mandala, and that accomplishes the form kayas of a buddha. The way that Luminosity Great Completion's path[60] makes both the dharma and form kayas manifest is as follows. The rigpa of the time of the ground that was introduced earlier is determined to be some-

[59] Close-taking is the particular step of setting in place the causes that determine a future birth. Usually it is setting up the next samsaric birth. In this case, it is setting up the birth of a deity.

[60] This is sometimes translated as "luminous path of Great Completion" or "luminous Great Completion's path". From the text so far, it should be very obvious that innermost Great Completion is the path of luminosity. Therefore, one of the many names it is given is Luminosity Great Completion. The other translations miss the point and take the listener in a wrong direction as well.

thing that has many wondrous dharmas associated with it, then meditation on rigpa's way of being seated, exactly as it is, is done. That accomplishes the wisdom dharmakāya. Then, although there is the ability to produce in that luminosity of the time of the ground the various appearances and various types of thinking and knowing, this is still a time at which it has not been awakened. When the ability to produce them at the time of ground appearances has been completed in its entirety, inconceivable kayas, bindus, arrangements of fields, and so on will shine forth whereby that luminosity of the time of the ground, present now in the mode of the ground of shining forth, is fully completed at the time of the ground appearances. It is determined like that using the path of Direct Crossing, then the force of familiarization is what accomplishes the aspects of the form kayas, which is the special feature of this path.

The system of unsurpassed mantra makes a path in accordance with what exists in the ground, therefore it is also quicker and works via that key point. That is also important in understanding why that sort of meditation or that sort of method of making things into the path is not explained in the Paramita Vehicle.

There is a similarity in the way that both Great Completion and Kalachakra accomplish the two form bodies based on "empty form" but it is not guaranteed that all aspects of their paths are the same in all ways. In Great Completion's own path, the ground of shining forth, the path, the particulars of the essentials[61], and so on, and the topics of path practice are not common but have many special, superior features. In Kalachakra, the ten signs[62] are taught but the four lamps, the four appearances, and so on[63] are not taught. In Great Completion, many special things such as the four lamps, and so on are taught but the ten signs of smoke, and so on and many of the related topics of path practice are not taught[64]. Thus, even though there is similarity just because of the way of shining forth of empty form, there are many sub-topics related to that which differ in many ways. Putting it this way, it is not hard to understand[65].

---

[61] Particulars of the essentials is the individual headings of all the essential topics that comprise the whole classification of the path.

[62] Of smoke and so forth that indicate the wind is entering the central channel. These signs show that the initial success needed is being obtained and that actual wisdom is starting to develop due to the practice. It is a major topic in the unsurpassed tantras of the new translation period and especially in Kalachakra.

[63] Which are the special features of Direct Crossing alone …

[64] There is an enormous amount of teaching connected with the appearance of the ten signs and then the steps that have to be gone through to get to the final fruition. This teaching is not present in Great Completion.

[65] What this comes down to is that both systems use the phrase "empty forms" but what it refers to is different and everything entailed in the paths to the development of their respective forms are very different. Empty forms for Direct Crossing refers to the appearances of form that arise during the four steps of the path called "the four appearances". Empty forms in Kalachakra refer

(continued...)

The factor of the time of the ground at which the ability to produce various thinkings and various appearances has not yet woken up on top of the rigpa itself taken as the practice by the Thorough Cut path is, in relation to making ground appearances into the path, a little slower. The factor of ground appearances where the ability of rigpa to produce its own various thinkings and appearances taken as the practice by the Direct Crossing path is, in relation to making ground into the path, extremely rapid. Thus, this point of the profoundly special awarenesses of the two also is a very important key point of path.

Again, in relation to the path of Great Completion, the paths of other unsurpassed mantra work the key points of the three of channels, drops, and winds so great-bliss wisdom is factored in but it is only a rough application that is involved. These paths that, in the beginning, work the key points of the channels, winds, and so on simply to make luminosity great-bliss wisdom manifest are extremely rapid but also have many flaws such taking a long time to arrive at final attainment, and so on. This path of Great Completion needs familiarization to be done for a long time, so that to begin with, the good qualities of the path signs are produced in mind, so it does

---

[65](...continued)
to something else entirely. This particular point has always been a subject of discussion amongst Great Completion practitioners. It is similar to the fact that there is the term "Direct Crossing" in the new translation tantras but what it refers to has nothing to do with the Direct Crossing of innermost Great Completion. When the words are seen, it sparks interest, and that leads to these types of discussions.

take a little longer than the other but, when the wisdom that comes from the familiarization has been produced in the mindstream, from the perspective of many factors such as the long time that the others take to get to vastness[66], and so on, this path is quicker and more profound, so it is a path that has many special features connected with its being the peak, the king of vehicles, and so on.

Now, I will give a short explanation of the presentation of Direct Crossing's subject that is specially cherished, the four lamps. Inside the central channel there is a channel not known in the other tantra sections called "the Kati Crystal Tube" which is not at all produced from blood and lymph and which is also called "Golden Sun Ocean". The two are in fact the same thing. That Kati Crystal Tube channel comes out from inside the central channel at the heart centre and splits into five. One end stays in the central channel and the other ends go into the crown, the two eyes, and the two ears. If any one of those channels can be opened, then all five will be opened, and if the mouth of any one of them is shut, all of

---

[66] The other paths are fast to start with because they have the means to manifest great bliss wisdom very quickly. However, after that, their techniques of channels, winds, and drops take a long time to bring the vast aspect of the wisdom to fruition. Great Completion on the other hand takes a little longer to make the great-bliss wisdom manifested sufficiently to be the starting point of the path but when that has happened, its techniques of Thorough Cut and Direct Crossing are vastly superior because they can take the practitioner to the fruition of the vast aspect in a much shorter time than the techniques of the other tantra sections.

their mouths will shut. Because of that, and to begin with, the technique for opening the mouth of the channel that is the path to the Far Reaching Lasso is shown.

Then, there are the four lamps: the lamp of the watery far-reaching lasso; the lamp of the completely pure expanse; the lamp of the empty bindu; and the lamp of the rigpa chains. The first is as follows. It is spoken of in terms of "a tubed channel of light that penetrates the eyeballs". Its outer face does not apprehend the impure factors of ordinary rocks, earth, and so on. Its inner face is only rigpa's way of being seated, deep luminosity, the youthful vase body. The second is as follows. The lamp of the completely pure expanse is the sky which, as the factor that opens the door, is the sky with an appearance of the blue lustre that is the sky's own colour. The third is as follows. The lamp of the empty bindu is, like a fish's eye, a bindu of five lights with azure blue centre. The fourth is as follows. The lamp of rigpa's chains is bindus and little bindus linked together like a fish hook or a golden thread of ten bindu knots.

If the lamp of rigpa's chains is categorized, there are the thing itself, the liveliness, and the offput. The thing itself is Thorough Cut's rigpa or, you can also say, rigpa self-arising wisdom. The liveliness is prajna, samadhi, dharani, confidence of knowledge, outpourings from the expanse of words and meaning, and so on. The offput is the offput rigpa vajra chains like a woven iron rope or ten-dropped knots and that is also called prajna self-arising lamp.

At the end, this is what occurs. When the lamp of the completely pure expanse has peaked, it will be the Densely Arrayed Akanishta field explained previously in the Rigpa Liveliness Empowerment[67]. When the lamp of the empty bindu has peaked, it will be the immeasurable mansion of the sambhogakāya. When the lamp of self-arising prajñā has peaked, it will be buddha as the sambhogakāya. When the thing itself or the liveliness has peaked, it will be buddha as the enlightened mind of the sambhogakāya, the wisdom knowledge that knows every superfice. When the dharmatā of self-sound has peaked, it will be buddha accomplished as the sambhogakāya speech with the sixty melodies of Brahma.

The practice of two paths of Thorough Cut and Direct Crossing can be summed up like this. The ground of alpha purity and Thorough Cut's way of rigpa being seated have the luminosity of death and becoming made into the basis of the feature. Then its features, which are each of its various different good qualities are shown from the perspective of the many features of rigpa such as alpha purity, transparency, freedom, primordial liberation, unaltered, spread everywhere, youthful vase body, and so on. Then, the fact that accords with that is introduced by the guru's foremost instructions and, having been introduced, is well acquainted with as one's own thinking mind and has to be made into a certainty. Then there is a decision on one thing, which is that this rigpa is not something that someone else has, it is rigpa that is one factor of this present awareness and which has the many features just explained. After that, with a mindfulness mindful of that rigpa's way of being seated that comes up all of a sudden and does not forget the rigpa for even a moment, and not with an

---

[67] Tib. rig pa'i rtsal dbang.

interest-type meditation that thinks, "This mind of the present has become the entity of rigpa" but within a state that comes from the decision that all of these factors of present awareness are rigpa only of uncompounded nature, meditation on the nature of rigpa's way of being seated is to be done, and that is the uncommon key point of meaning belonging to this context. That is not a meditation of exaggeration in which what is not is taken to be what is; that is having been introduced by the guru's foremost instructions to what primordially is as what is then meditating using this path—this understanding also is another one of the key points involved.

At the time of Direct Crossing, the meaning of "rigpa is aimed at the eye" is this. The way that the channels of the vajra body have amongst them a channel of light not known in the other unsurpassed tantra sections called "Kati Crystal Tube, Golden Sun Ocean" which exists inside the central channel and one end of which pierces to the centre of the eyeball is first nicely introduced using the guru's foremost instructions. Following that, one has to come to a good and definite understanding of that channel just as it was introduced. Then, one has to gain good understanding of how all the appearances of the three of expanse, bindu, and rigpa shine forth within that channel and, having done that, the ground alpha purity's rigpa is aimed at the eye. The eye is aimed at the lamp of the completely pure expanse up in space and at the rigpa vajra chains, then the preservation of superficies of the three of expanse, rigpa, and bindu, with rigpa not being discarded for even an instant, is undertaken; this is the uncommon path of Direct Crossing. To begin with, one makes that kind of shining forth[68] occur in relation to an object condition of the sun, moon, and butter lamp, whichever is appropriate, and one familiarizes oneself well with the appearances of expanse and bindu. After that, if that channel of light awakens at some point, then, without needing to relate to an object condition, inconceivable appearances of empty forms will be made to shine forth in the expanse of the light channel itself. This initial having to rely on an outer object condition and then, when familiarization has been done for a long time, not having to rely on an outer object condition, is like a clay pot cured by heat.

At the time of Direct Crossing, "rigpa" is used to refer to the lamp of the rigpa chains that has the three points of the thing itself, liveliness, and offput. The thing itself, rigpa of the empty side is called "alpha purity, Thorough Cut's rigpa". The offput, rigpa of the appearing side is called "spontaneous presence Direct Crossing's rigpa vajra chains". The liveliness is called "the lamp of self-arising rigpa" or, from the aspect of the outpouring of words and meaning from the expanse, is called "the lamp of self-arising prajñā". All three of these in this context here are given the term "rigpa".

The appearance experiences that are the appearance part of Direct Crossing and the knowledge experiences that are the rigpa of Thorough Cut are only ever classed as two things

---

[68] Shining forth is a specific techinical term that refers to appearances that come forth in mind itself.

whose difference is that they are facets of one entity[69]; like the sun and its rays, they mutually assist and accompany each other until ultimately the appearance experiences become buddha's form kayas and the knowledge experiences become buddha's wisdom, the dharmakāya. Thus the two are the particulars that are facets of one entity, for example like fire and heat, water and wetness.

At the time of exhaustion of dharmas, "the external level earth, stones, rocky mountains, and so on end, the internal level heap of elements ends, the secret level mass of mind's thoughts ends, and the very secret level Direct Crossing's appearance part ends", all of which is called "the dharmatā exhaustion point". The first is that, for the yogin who has made it as far as dharmatā exhaustion point, since he has reached the end of the path's journey, the latencies that cause the appearance of the things of impurity—earth, stones, rocky mountains and so on, have definitely been ended so the external objects of earth, stones, rocky mountains, and so on also have ended. The second is that the latencies that cause the appearance of this body which is a thing of impurity at the internal level have definitely been ended so the "internal heap of elements" has ended. Third is that the mass of thoughts moved by the wind coming from total concept or the ability to create the elaborations of grasped-grasping have definitely ended so the secret level mass of mind's thoughts has ended.

---

[69] This is a specific philosophical classification. There are four types of differences that indicate the exact way in which two or more items are related to and or different from each other. The name of the one that is operative here, "the difference of being different facets of one entity", speaks for itself.

Fourth is that all the appearance portion of spontaneous existence Direct Crossing, the movement producing winds or latencies have definitely been ended so all of the very secret level Direct Crossing's appearance part ends.

In this context, "exhaustion" has the meaning "to flow back in" so, even though there is definitely nothing more[70] beyond this total completion of the liveliness of all the Direct Crossing appearance part, the movement causing winds having been exhausted with nothing left to go, all of the appearance part of spontaneous appearance Direct Crossing flows back into, or is sealed within, the dharma dhātu. There is an equipoise that has the mode of not arising from the dharmatā of suchness' dharmadhātu and while that continues on, the two form kāyas effortlessly, spontaneously fulfill all of the hopes that are the desires of sentient beings to be tamed; the term dharmatā tells the story of the primordial guardian[71] who has the ability to do that. The ultimate accomplishment of unified enlightened body and mind like that is the ultimate accomplishment of form body or unification body of no more training[72] that is a unification of the superfice that is the

---

[70] Of path ...

[71] Primordial guardian is a name for the Samantabhadra that is a being who has achieved this level.

[72] Mahamudra and Great Completion both point out that their paths are paths of unification and that the fruition of those paths is unification. Sometimes they mix the sutra teaching of the five paths with that, a teaching in which the final path is buddhahood and is called "the path of no more learning". Hence you get "the

(continued...)

display of the form body and the entity that is wisdom that knows all superficies.

The three of entity, nature, and compassionate activity are like this. The primordially liberated, uncompounded rigpa is said to be "the entity empty" given that it has not so much as a speck of being existent by way of self-entity, by way of own nature. Here, "entity" is in relation to the fact that, all of the elaborations of grasped-grasping which are factors of the movement of karmic winds, total conceptuality, have been purified, so are absent or empty[73].

The nature, luminosity, does not mean something like all factors of illumination-knowing have become definitely absent rather, it means that rigpa's nature is such that there is no stoppage in the illumination that comprises it; rigpa's nature has an aspect of crystal clear bliss; it has no delimitations of any sort in it; it has no falling at all into sides in it. To go further with that, "has no delimitations of any sort in it" means that, because all the factors associated with the rigpa offput are a realm empty in that they are free from all

---

[72](...continued)
unification body (and so on) of no more training".

[73] In Buddhism in general, since Buddha made emptiness the foremost teaching, the one that has to come before any discussion of appearance that comes from the emptiness and how to work with it, "the entity" is always equated with the empty factor and then nature and so on, are equated with the appearances of that emptiness. Hence, you first have entity, that is followed by the nature, then the function of the two; they are emptiness, luminosity, and all-pervading compassionate activity.

apprehensions of measurement, a realm that is everywhere spread, it is undelimited. That rigpa not falling into sides of a blissful fragment and a suffering fragment, its nature is one of being the great all-pervading spread, therefore, it is the nature luminosity.

"All-pervasive compassionate activity" is as follows. Generally, "compassionate activity" is explained to mean compassion but in this case here, it is rigpa that has become the ground of shining forth that has with it the inanimate and animate, containers and contents, so it has to be understood to mean that it is rigpa's liveliness or rigpa's gadgetry or miracles. Because there being nowhere in either samsara or nirvana that it does not pervade, it holds the life of both samsara and nirvana, and because it reverses following after existence and non-existence, it is the all-pervasive compassionate activity.

Footnote in the woodblock: When the lord guru was young and gave this explanation to a group of people, I wrote it down in a set of notes that followed his order of explanation. This is not how people speak about this subject these days and I could not find an authenticating text for it but I did write it down according to what I understood the lord guru gave at the group's request, corrected it, and had it printed[74].

---

[74] For more explanation of the woodblock colophon, see the introduction.

GLOSSARY

Actuality, Tib. gnas lugs: A key term in both sutra and tantra and one of a pair of terms, the other being apparent reality (Tib. snang lugs). The two terms are used when determining the reality of a situation. The actuality of any given situation is how (lugs) the situation actuality sits or is present (gnas); the apparent reality is how any given situation appears to an observer. Something could appear in many different ways, depending on the circumstances at the time and on the being perceiving it but, regardless of those circumstances, it will always have its own actuality, how it really is. The term actuality is frequently used in Mahāmudrā and Great Completion teachings to mean the fundamental reality of any given phenomenon or situation before any deluded mind alters it and makes it appear differently.

Affliction, Skt. kleśha, Tib. nyon mongs: This term is usually translated as emotion or disturbing emotion, etcetera but Buddha was very specific about the meaning of this word. When the Buddha referred to the emotions, meaning a movement of mind, he did not refer to them as such but called them "kleśha" in Sanskrit, meaning exactly "affliction". It is a basic part of the Buddhist teaching that emotions afflict beings, giving them problems at the time and causing more problems in the future.

Alaya, Tib. kun gzhi: This term, if translated, is usually translated as all-base or thereabouts. It is a Sanskrit term that means a range that underlies and forms a basis for something else. In Buddhist teaching, it means a particular level of mind that sits beneath all other levels of mind. However, it is used in several different ways in the Buddhist teaching and changes to a different meaning in case. In the Great Completion teachings, a distinction is made between alaya and alaya consciousness; the distinction is subtle but the two must not be confused.

Alpha purity, Tib. ka dag: A Great Completion term meaning purity that is there from the first, that is, primordial purity. There are many terms in Buddhism that express the notion of "primordial purity" but this one is unique to the Great Completion teaching. Some people do not like the term "alpha purity" but this is exactly what the Tibetan says.

Bliss, clarity, and no-thought, Tib. bde gsal mi rtog pa: A practitioner who engages in practice will have signs of that practice appear as various types of temporary experience. Most commonly, three types of experience are met with: bliss, clarity, and no-thought. Bliss is ease of the body and-or mind, clarity is heightened knowing of mind, and no-thought is an absence of thought that happens in the mind. The three are usually mentioned when discussing the passing experiences that arise because of practising meditation but there is also a way of describing them as final experiences of realization.

Clarity or Illumination, Skt. vara, Tib. gsal ba: When you see this term, it should be understood as an abbreviation of the full term in Tibetan, 'od gsal ba, which is usually translated as luminosity. It is not another factor of mind distinct from luminosity but merely a convenient abbreviation in both Indian and Tibetan dharma language for the longer term, luminosity. See "Luminosity" in this glossary for more.

Clinging, Tib. zhen pa: In Buddhism, this term refers specifically to the twofold process of dualistic mind mis-taking things that are not true, not pure, as true, pure, etcetera and then, because of seeing them as highly desirable even though they are not, attaching itself to or clinging to those things. This type of clinging acts as a kind of glue that keeps you with the unsatisfactory things of cyclic existence because of mistakenly seeing them as desirable.

Complexion, Tib. mdangs: In both Mahāmudrā and Great Completion there is the general term "offput" (Tib. gdangs) meaning what is given off by something, for example the sound given off by a loudspeaker. There is another Tibetan word spelled "mdangs" instead of "gdangs". The Mahāmudrā teaching makes no difference between the two terms but Great Completion teachings does make a distinction. In great completion this term spelled "mdangs" has the special meaning not of the general output or offput coming from something but of the "complexion" of thing. It is a more subtle meaning. In Great Completion it conveys not just the sense of what is given off by the emptiness factor of mind in general (which would be its offput and which is talked about, too) but specifically means the complexion of the emptiness or, you could also say, its lustre.

Confusion, Tib. 'khrul pa: In Buddhism, this term mostly refers to the fundamental confusion of taking things the wrong way that happens because of fundamental ignorance though it can also have the more general meaning of having lots of thoughts and being confused about it. In the first case, it is defined like this, "Confusion is the appearance to rational mind of something being present when it is not", and refers for example to seeing an object, such as a table, as being truly present when in fact it is present only as mere, interdependent appearance.

Contrivance, contrived, Tib. bcos pa: A term meaning that something has been altered from its native state.

Cyclic existence, Skt. saṃsāra, Tib. 'khor ba: The type of existence that sentient beings have which is that they continue on from one existence to another, always within the enclosure of births that are produced by ignorance and experienced as unsatisfactory. Although the Tibetan term literally means "cycling", the original Sanskrit has a slightly different meaning; it means to go about, here and there.

Dharmakaya, Tib. chos sku: The mind of a buddha. Dharma here means reality, what actually is, and kāya means body.

Dharmata, Tib. chos nyid: A Sanskrit term used to refer to the reality of any given situation. Thus, there are many dharmatās. The term is often used in Buddhism to refer to general reality that underlies all types of existence but that is not its only meaning. For example, even the fact of water's wetness can be referred to as the dharmatā of water, meaning water's reality in general. The term is similar to "actuality" (Tib. gnas lugs).

Dhyana, Tib. bsam gtan: A Sanskrit term meaning all types of mental absorption. Mental absorptions cultivated in the human realm generally result in births in the form realms which are deep forms of concentration in themselves. The practices of mental absorption done in the human realm and the godly existences of the form realm that result from them both are named "dhyāna". The Buddha repeatedly pointed out that the dhyānas were a side-track to emancipation from cyclic existence.

Direct Crossing, Tib. tho rgal: The name of the two main practices of the innermost level of Great Completion. The other one is Thorough Cut.

Discursive thought, Skt. vikalpita, Tib. rnam rtog: This means more than just the superficial thought that is heard as a voice in the head. It includes the entirety of conceptual process that arises due to mind contacting any object of any of the senses. The Sanskrit and Tibetan literally mean "(dualistic) thought (that arises from the mind wandering among the) various (superficies perceived in the doors of the senses)".

Elaboration, Tib. spro ba: to be producing thoughts.

Entity, Tib. ngo bo: The entity of something is just exactly what that thing is. In English we would often simply say "thing" rather than entity but there is the problem that, in Buddhism, "thing" has a very specific meaning and not the general meaning that it has in English. See also under Essence in this glossary.

Equipoise and post-attainment, Tib. mnyam bzhag and rjes thob: Although often called "meditation and post-meditation", the actual term is "equipoise and post-attainment". There is great meaning in the actual wording which is lost by the looser translation.

Exaggeration, Tib. skur 'debs pa: In Buddhism, this term is used in two ways. Firstly, it is used in general to mean misunderstanding from the perspective that one has added more to one's understanding of something than needs to be there. Secondly, it is used specifically to indicate that dualistic mind always overstates or exaggerates whatever object it is examining. Dualistic mind always adds the ideas of solidity, permanence, singularity, and so on to everything it references via the concepts that it uses. Severing of exaggeration either means removal of these un-necessary understandings when trying to properly comprehend something or removal of the dualistic process altogether when trying to get to the non-dualistic reality of a phenomenon.

Expanse, Skt. dhātu, Tib. dbyings: A Sanskrit term with over twenty meanings to it. Many of those meanings are also present in the Tibetan equivalent. In the Vajra Vehicle teachings it is used as a replacement for the term emptiness that conveys a non-theoretical sense of the experience of emptiness. When used this way, it has the sense "expanse" because emptiness is experienced as an expanse in which all phenomena appear.

Fictional, Skt. saṃvṛti, Tib. kun rdzob: This term is paired with the term "superfactual" q.v. Until now these two terms have been translated as "relative" and "absolute" but the translations are nothing like the original terms. These terms are extremely important in the Buddhist teaching so it is very important that they be corrected but more than that, if the actual meaning of these terms is not presented, then the teaching connected with them cannot be understood.

The Sanskrit term saṃvṛti means a deliberate invention, a fiction, a hoax. It refers to the mind of ignorance which, because of being obscured and so not seeing suchness, is not true but a fiction. The things that appear to the ignorance are therefore fictional. Nonetheless, the beings who live in this ignorance believe that the things that appear to them through the filter of ignorance are true, are real. Therefore, these beings live in fictional truth.

Fictional truth, Skt. saṃvṛtisatya, Tib. kun rdzob bden pa: See under "Fictional" for an explanation of this term.

Foremost instruction, Skt. upadeśha, Tib. man ngag: there are several types of instruction mentioned in Buddhist literature: there is the general level of instruction which is the meaning contained in the words of the texts of the tradition; on a more personal and direct level there is oral instruction which has been passed down from teacher to student from the time of the buddha; and on the most profound level there is upadeśha which are not only oral instructions provided by one's guru but are special, core instructions that come out of personal experience and which convey the teaching concisely and with the full weight of personal experience. Upadeśha are crucial to the Vajra Vehicle because these are the special way of passing on the profound instructions needed for the student's realization.

Grasped-grasping, Tib. gzung 'dzin: When mind is turned outwardly as it is in the normal operation of dualistic mind, it has developed two faces that appear simultaneously. Special names are given to these two faces: mind appearing in the form of the external object being referenced is called "that which is grasped". Mind appearing in the form of the consciousness that is referencing it is called "the grasper" or "grasping" of it. Thus, there is the pair of terms "grasped-grasper" or "grasped-grasping". When these two terms are used, it alerts you immediately to the fact that a Mind Only style of presentation is being discussed. This pair of terms pervades Mind Only, Madhyamaka, and tantric writings and is exceptionally important in all of them.

Note that you could substitute the word "apprehended" for "grasped" and "apprehender" for "grasper" or "grasping" and that would reflect one connotation of the original Indian terminology. The solidified duality of grasped and grasper is nothing but an invention of dualistic thought. It has that kind of character or characteristic.

Ground, Tib. gzhi: This is the first member of the formulation of ground, path, and fruition. Ground, path, and fruition is the way that the teachings of the path of oral instruction belonging to the Vajra Vehicle are presented to students. Ground refers to the basic situation as it is.

Introduction and To Introduce, Tib. ngos sprad and ngos sprod pa respectively: This pair of terms is usually translated in the

U.S.A. these days as "pointing out" "and "to point out" but this is a mistake that has, unfortunately, become entrenched. The terms are the standard terms used in day to day life for the situation in which one person introduces another person to someone or something. They are the exact same words as our English "introduction" and "to introduce".

In the Vajra Vehicle, these terms are specifically used for the situation in which one person introduces another person to the nature of his own mind. Now there is a term in Tibetan for "pointing out" but that term is never used for this purpose because in this case no-one points out anything. Rather, a person is introduced by another person to a part of himself that he has forgotten about.

Key points, Tib. gnad: Key points are those places in one's being that one works, like pressing buttons, in order to get some desired effect. For example, in meditation, there are key points of the body; by adjusting those key points, the mind is brought closer to reality and the meditation is thus assisted.

In general, this term is used in Buddhist meditation instruction but it is, in particular, part of the special vocabulary of the Great Completion teachings. Overall, the Great Completion teachings are given as a series of key points that must be attended to in order to bring forth the various realizations of the path.

Latency, Skt. vāsana, Tib. bag chags: The Sanskrit term means a karmic seed that has been imprinted on the mindstream and is present there as a latency that could, in the future, manifest. Although it has become popular to translate this term as "habitual pattern", that is not its meaning. Some latencies might belong to habitual patterns of a being but not all will be that way. The key meaning of the original, Sanskrit term is "latency", something sitting there in mind, ready and waiting to come into manifestation.

Liveliness, Tib. rtsal: A key term in both Mahāmudrā and Great Completion. The term means the ability that something has to express itself. In the case of rigpa, it refers to how the rigpa actually comes out into expression. The term is sometimes translated as "display" but that is not right. It is not merely the display that is being talked about here but the fact that something has the ability to express itself in a certain way. Another English word that fits the meaning, though one which is much drier than "liveliness" is "expressivity". In the end, given the way that this term is actually used in the higher tantras, it refers to the liveliness of whatever is being referred to, usually rigpa.

Luminosity, Skt. prabhāsvara, Tib. 'od gsal ba: the core of mind, called mind's essence, has two aspects, parts, or factors as they are called. One is emptiness and the other is knowing. Luminosity is a metaphor for the fundamental knowing quality of the essence of mind. It is sometimes translated as "clear light" but that is a mistake that comes from not understanding how the words of the Sanskrit and the Tibetan, too, go together. It does not refer to a light that has the quality of clearness (something that makes no sense, actually!) but refers to the illuminative property which is the hallmark of mind. Mind knows, that is what it does. Metaphorically, it is a luminosity that illuminates its own content. In both Sanskrit and Tibetan Buddhist literature, the term is frequently abbreviated just to gsal ba, "clarity", with the same meaning.

Mind, Skt. chitta, Tib. sems: the complicated process of mind which occurs because there is ignorance. This sort of mind is a samsaric phenomenon. It is a dualistic mind.

Mindfulness, Tib. dran pa: A particular mental event, one that has the ability to keep mind on its object. Together with alertness, it is one of the two causes of developing shamatha. See alertness for a explanation.

Not stopped, Tib. ma 'gags pa: An important path term in the teaching of both Mahāmudrā and Great Completion. The essence of mind has two parts: emptiness and luminosity. Both of these must come unified. However, when a practitioner does the practice, he will fall into one extreme or the other and that is called "stoppage". The aim of the practice is to get to the stage in which there is both emptiness and luminosity together. In that case, there is no stoppage of falling into one extreme or the other. Thus non-stopped luminosity is a term that indicates that there is the luminosity with all of its appearance yet that luminosity, for the practitioner, is not mistaken, is not stopped off. Stopped luminosity is an experience like luminosity but in which the appearances have, at least to some extent, not been mixed with emptiness.

Offput, Tib. gdangs: A general Tibetan term meaning that which is given off by something else, for example, the sound that comes from a loudspeaker. In Mahāmudrā and Great Completion, it the general term used to refer to what is given off by the emptiness factor of the essence of mind. Emptiness is the empty condition of the essence of mind, like space. However, that emptiness has liveliness and liveliness comes off it as compassion and all the other qualities of enlightened mind, and, equally, all the apparatus of dualistic mind. All of this collectively is called its offput. Note that the Great Completion teachings have a special word that is a more refined version of this term; see "complexion" for that.

Outflow, Skt. saśrava, Tib. zag pa: Outflows occur when wisdom loses its footing and falls into the elaborations of dualistic mind. Therefore, anything with duality also has outflows. This is sometimes translated as "defiled" or "conditioned" but these fail to capture the meaning. The idea is that wisdom can remain self-contained in its own unique sphere but, when it loses its ability to stay within itself, it starts to have leakages into dualism that are defilements on the wisdom. See also un-outflowed.

Post-attainment, Tib. rjes thob: see "Equipoise and post-attainment".

Prajna, Tib. shes rab: A Sanskrit term for the type of mind that makes good and precise distinctions between this and that and hence which arrives at good understanding. It is sometimes translated as "wisdom" but that is not correct because it is, generally speaking, a mental event belonging to dualistic mind where "wisdom" is generally used to refer to the non-dualistic knower of a Buddha. Moreover, the main feature of prajna is its ability to distinguish correctly between one thing and another and hence to have a good understanding. It is very much part of intellect.

Preserve, Tib. skyong ba: An important term in both Mahāmudrā and Great Completion. In general, it means to defend, protect, nurture, maintain. In the higher tantras it means to keep something just as it is, to nurture that something so that it stays and is not lost. Also, in the higher tantras, it is often used in reference to preserving the state where the state is some particular state of being. Because of this, the phrase "preserve the state" is an important instruction in the higher tantras.

Rational mind, Tib. blo: The Kagyu and Nyingma traditions use this term pejoratively for the most part. In the Great Completion and Mahāmudrā teachings, this term specifically means the dualistic mind. It is the villain, so to speak, which needs to be removed from the equation in order to obtain enlightenment. This term is commonly translated simply as mind but that causes confusion with the many other words that are also translated simply as mind. It is not just another mind but is specifically the sort of mind that creates the situation of this and that (ratio in Latin) and hence upholds the duality of samsara. It is the very opposite of the essence of mind. Thus, this is a key term which should be noted and not just glossed over as "mind".

Rigpa, Tib. rig pa: This is the singularly most important term in the whole of Great Completion and Mahāmudrā. In particular, it is the key word of all words in the Great Completion system of the Thorough Cut. Rigpa literally means to know in the sense of "I see!" It is used at all levels of meaning from the coarsest everyday sense of knowing something to the deepest sense of knowing something as presented in the system of Thorough Cut. The system of Thorough Cut uses this term in a very special sense, though it still retains its basic meaning of "to know". To translate it as "awareness" which is common practice these days is a poor practice; there are many kinds of awareness but there is only one rigpa and besides, rigpa is substantially more than just awareness. Since this is such an important term and since it lacks an equivalent in English, I choose not to translate it. However, it will be helpful in reading the text to understanding the meaning as just given.

This is the term used to indicate enlightened mind as experienced by the practitioner on the path of these practices. The term itself specifically refers to the dynamic knowing quality of mind. It absolutely does not mean a simple registering, as implied by the word "awareness" which unfortunately is often used to translate this term. There is no word in English that exactly matches it, though the idea of "seeing" or "insight on the spot" is very close. Proof of this is found in the fact that the original Sanskrit term "vidyā" is actually the root of all words in English that start with "vid" and mean "to see", for example, "video", "vision", and so on. Chogyam Trungpa Rinpoche, who was particular skilled at getting Tibetan words into English, also stated that this term rigpa really did not have a good equivalent in English, though he thought that "insight" was the closest. My own conclusion after hearing extensive teaching on it is that rigpa is just best left untranslated. However, it will be helpful in reading the text to understanding the meaning as just given. Note that rigpa has both noun and verb forms. To get the verb form, I use "rigpa'ing".

Secret Mantra, Tib. gsang sngags: Another name for the Vajra Vehicle or the tantric teachings.

Shamatha, Tib. gzhi gnas: The name of one of the two main practices of meditation used in the Buddhist system to gain insight into reality. This practice creates a foundation of one-pointedness of mind which can then be used to focus the insight of the other practice, vipaśhyanā. If the development of shamatha is taken through to completion, the result is a mind that sits stably on its object without any effort and a body which is filled with ease. Altogether, this result of the practice is called "the creation of workability of body and mind".

State, Tib. ngang: A key term in Mahāmudrā and Great Completion. Unfortunately it is often not translated and in so doing much meaning is lost. Alternatively, it is often translated as "within" which is incorrect. The term means a "state". A state is a certain, ongoing situation. In Buddhist meditation in general, there are various states that a practitioner has to enter and remain in as part of developing the meditation.

Stoppageless, Tib. 'gag pa med pa: A key term in Mahāmudrā and Great Completion. It is usually translated as "unceasing" but this is a different verb. It refers to the situation in which one thing is not being stopped by another thing. It means "not stopped", "without stoppage", "not blocked and prevented by something else" that is, stoppageless. The verb form associated with it is "not stopped" q.v. It is used in relation to the practice of luminosity. A stoppageless luminosity is the actual state of reality and what the practitioner has to aim for. At the beginning of the practice, a practitioner's experience of luminosity will usually not be stoppageless but with stoppages.

Superfactual, Skt. paramārtha,Tib. don dam: This term is paired with the term "fictional" q.v. Until now these two terms have been translated as "relative" and "absolute" but those translations are nothing like the original terms. These terms are extremely important in the Buddhist teaching so it is very important that their translations be corrected but, more than that, if the actual meaning of these terms is not presented, the teaching connected with them cannot be understood.

The Sanskrit term parāmartha literally means "a superior or holy kind of fact" and refers to the wisdom mind possessed by those who have developed themselves spiritually to the point of having transcended samsara. That wisdom is *superior* to an ordinary, un-developed person's consciousness and the *facts* that appear on its surface are superior compared to the facts that appear on the ordinary person's consciousness. Therefore, it is superfact or the holy fact, more literally. What this wisdom sees is true for the beings who have it, therefore what the wisdom sees is superfactual truth.

Superfactual truth, Skt. paramārthasatya, Tib. don dam bden pa: see under "Superfactual" for an explanation of this term.

Superfice, superficies, Tib. rnam pa: in discussions of mind, a distinction is made between the entity of mind which is a mere knower and the superficial things that appear on its surface and which are known by it. In other words, the superficies are the various things which pass over the surface of mind but which are not mind. Superficies are all the specifics that constitute appearance, for example, the colour white within a moment of visual consciousness, the sound heard within an ear consciousness, and so on.

Thorough Cut, Tib. khregs chod: the Dzogchen system has several levels to it. The innermost level has two main practices, the first called Thregcho which literally translates as Thorough Cut and the second called Thogal which translates as Direct Crossing. The meaning of Thorough Cut has been misunderstood. The meaning is clearly explained in the *Illuminator Tibetan-English Dictionary*:

> "Thorough Cut is a practice in which the solidification that sentient beings produce by having rational minds which grasp at a perceived object and perceiving subject is sliced through so as to get the underlying reality which has always been present in the essence of mind and which is called Alpha Purity in this system of teachings. For this reason, Thorough Cut is also known as Alpha Purity Thorough Cut."

The etymology of the word is explained in the Great Completion teachings either as ཁྲེགས་སུ་ཆོད་པ་ or ཁྲེགས་གེ་ཆོད་པ་. In either case, the term ཆོད་པ་ is "a cut"; there are all sorts of different "cuts" and this is one of them. Then, in the case of ཁྲེགས་སུ་ཆོད་པ་, ཁྲེགས་སུ་ is an adverb modifying the verb "to cut" and has the meaning of making the cut fully, completely. It is explained with the example of slicing off a finger. A finger could be sliced with a sharp knife such that the cut was not quite complete and the cut off portion was left hanging. Alternatively, it could be sliced through in one, decisive movement such that the finger was completely and definitely severed. That kind of thorough cut is what is meant here. In the case of ཁྲེགས་གེ་ཆོད་པ་, the term ཁྲེགས་གེ་ is as an adverb that has the meaning of something that is doubtless, of something that is unquestionably so. A translation based on the first explanation would be "Thorough Cut" and on the second would be "Decisive Cut".

Other translations that have been put forward for this term are: "Cutting Resistance" and "Cutting Solidity". Of these, "Cutting Resistance" is usually a translation made on the basis of students expressing the "resistance to practice", etcetera. That is a complete misunderstanding of the term. The term means that that the practitioner of this system cuts *decisively* through rational mind, regardless of its degree of solidity, so as to arrive directly at the essence of mind.

Transparency, Tib. zang thal: This term belongs to the unique vocabulary of Great Completion. It has two connotations: that something is seen directly, in direct perception; and that it is seen with full visibility because there is no agent obscuring the view of it. The term is used to indicate that rigpa is truly present for the practitioner. Luminosity when it is the rigpa of the enlightened side and not the not-rigpa, usually translated as ignorance, of the samsaric side, has transparency or, you could say, full visibility, as one of its qualities precisely because it has none of the factors of mind as such in it, which would obscure it. Transparency means that the rigpa is in full view: it really is rigpa seen in direct perception and it is without rational mind so it is seen without any of the obscuring factors that would make it less than immediately and fully visible.

Unaltered or uncontrived, Tib. ma bcos pa: The opposite of "altered" and "contrived". Something which has not been altered from its native state; something which has been left just as it is.

Un-outflowed, Skt. aśrava, Tib. zag pa med pa: See also "outflowed". Un-outflowed dharmas are ones that are connected with wisdom that has not lost its footing and leaked out into a defiled state; it is self-contained wisdom without any taint of dualistic mind and its apparatus.

Upadesha, Tib. man ngag: See the glossary entry "Foremost Instruction".

Vipashyana, Tib. lhag mthong: The Sanskrit name for one of the two main practices of meditation needed in the Buddhist system for gaining insight into reality. The other one, shamatha, keeps the mind focussed while this one, vipaśhyanā, looks piercingly into the nature of things.

Wisdom, Skt. jñāna, Tib. ye shes: This is a fruition term that refers to the kind of mind, the kind of knower possessed by a buddha. The original Sanskrit term has many meanings but overall has the sense of just knowing. In Buddhism, it refers to the most basic type of knowing possible. Sentient beings could do this but their minds are obscured so, although they have the potential for knowing with the wisdom of a buddha, it does not happen. If they practise the path to buddhahood, at some point they will leave behind their obscuration and start knowing in this very simple and immediate way.

This sort of knowing is there at the core of every being's mind. Therefore, the Tibetans called it "the particular type of awareness which is always there". Because of their wording, it is often called "primordial wisdom" but that is too much. It simply means wisdom in the sense of the most fundamental knowing possible.

TIBETAN TEXT

༄༅། །ཚིག་གསུམ་གནད་བརྡེག་སྐོར། །མཆོག་གསུམ་ཡོངས་འདུས་བླ་མའི་ཞབས་ལ་གུས་པ་ཆེན་པོས་ཕྱག་འཚལ་ལོ། །དེ་ལ་འདིར་འོད་གསལ་སྒྲོང་སྤོབས་ཀྱིས་མངོན་དུ་འགྱུར་བར་བྱེད་པ་ལ་ལམ་གྱི་སྒོམ་ཚུལ་གཉིས་ཡོད་པ་ལས། བླ་མེད་ཀྱི་རྒྱུད་སྡེ་གཞན་གྱི་རྩ་ཐིག་རླུང་གསུམ་ལ་གནད་དུ་བསྣུན་ནས་མངོན་དུ་འགྱུར་ཚུལ་ནི། དང་པོ་ནས་འོད་གསལ་གྱི་རྣམ་པ་བཤད་མི་དགོས་པ་སྙིང་གའམ་ལྟེ་བའི་རྩ་འཁོར་སོགས་ལ་གནད་དུ་བསྣུན་ན་འོད་གསལ་ཤར་འོང་། །འོད་གསལ་ཤར་བའི་ཚེ་ཡུལ་སྣང་ཐམས་ཅད་བདེ་བ་ཆེན་པོར་འཆར་བའི་གང་ཟག་ཁྱད་པར་བ་དེས་མཉམ་བཞག་གི་འོད་གསལ་དེ་ཉིད་རྗེས་ཐོབ་ཏུ་དྲན་པར་བྱེད་པའི་སྤོབས་ཀྱིས་ཀྱང་འོད་གསལ་དྲང་ཡོང་། དེའི་རྒྱུ་མཚན་ནི་དཔེར་ན་མའི་བུ་གཅིག་པུ་ཤི་ན་མ་དེ་སྡུག་བསྔལ་གྱིས་གདུང་བས་སྐྱིད་མོའི་ཚལ་ལ་སོགས་པའི་ཉམས་དགའི་གནས་སུ་ཕྱིན་ན་དགའ་བར་མི་འགྱུར་ལ་གང་དུ་ཕྱིན་ཀྱང་སྡུག་བསྔལ་བའི་རྣམ་པ་མ་གཏོགས་བདེ་བའི་རྣམ་པ་ནི་མི་འབྱུང་། དེ་བཞིན་དུ་མི་ནོར་ལ་སྲེད་སེམས་ཅན་གྱི་ལག་ཏུ་ཡིད་བཞིན་ནོར་བུ་རྙེད་ན་མི་དེའི་སེམས་དགའ་བའི་ཆོས་མདོག་གིས་བསྒྱུར་

ཡོད་པས་མི་དེ་རྟ་རྫང་ངམ་རྟའི་ར་བའི་ནང་དུ་འདུག་ཀྱང་དགའ་བའི་རྣམ་པ་མ་གཏོགས་སྡུག་བསྔལ་བའི་རྣམ་པ་མི་འབྱུང་། དེ་ལྟར་མཉམ་བཞག་གི་སྐབས་སུ་བདེ་བ་ཆེན་པོའི་ཡེ་ཤེས་ལ་གོམས་འདྲིས་ཡོད་པས་ན་ཕྱིས་རྗེས་ཐོབ་ཀྱི་སྐབས་སུ་རྩ་ཐིག་རླུང་ལ་གནད་དུ་བསྣུན་མི་དགོས་པར་བདེ་བ་ཆེན་པོའི་ཡེ་ཤེས་དེའི་རྣམ་པ་དྲན་ཙམ་གྱིས་དེ་ཉིད་འདྲེན་ཐུབ། རྫོགས་པ་ཆེན་པོའི་ལམ་ལ་དེ་ལྟར་རྩ་ཐིག་རླུང་སོགས་ལྷག་པར་བསྒོམ་མི་དགོས་པར། དང་པོ་བླ་མའི་མན་ངག་ལ་བརྟེན་ནས་རིག་པ་ཐུ་རེ་དྲན་པ་རྒྱུན་ཆགས་སུ་བསྐྱེན་པ་ནི་རིག་པའི་སྐྱོང་ཚུལ་ཡིན། དེ་ལ་བླ་མའི་མན་ངག་ནི་འཆི་སྲིད་ཀྱི་འོད་གསལ་དེ་ཉིད་ཚེ་འདིའི་སྣང་སེམས་ཐམས་ཅད་སྡུད་ས་དང་ཕྱི་མའི་སྣང་བ་ཐམས་ཅད་མཆེད་སའི་གཞི་ལྟ་བུ་ཡིན་ལ། དེ་ཀ་རང་འོད་གསལ་ཐམས་ཅད་སྟོང་པའམ་ཡེ་གྲོལ་འདུས་མ་བྱས་ཀྱི་རིག་པ་ཡིན། དེ་ནི་སྣང་མཆེད་ཀྱི་མཐའི་ཤེས་པ་ཕྲ་མོ་སྟེ། དེ་ལ་རིག་པའམ་འོད་གསལ་ཟེར། འོད་གསལ་དེ་ལ་འགྱུར་བ་ཡེ་ནས་ཡོད་མ་མྱོང་། བློ་བུར་བའི་སེམས་རིག་པ་དེའི་གཤིས་སུ་ཞུགས་མ་མྱོང་བ་ཡིན། བློ་བུར་བའི་སེམས་ཞེས་པ་ནི། བློ་བུར་དུ་སྐྱེས་པའི་ཤེས་པ་སྟེ། དབང་ཤེས་དང་དེ་ལས་ཕྲ་བའི་ཡིད་ཤེས་རྣམས་ཡིན། འོད་གསལ་དེའི་རྣམ་པ་ནི་ཡེ་གདོད་མ་ནས་བློ་བུར་བའི་རྐྱེན་གྱིས་གཤིས་མ་བསླད་པས་ན་ཀ་དག་ཟེར། ཀ་སྣོན་སུམ་ཅུའི་བཞུགས་ཚུལ་འཆུག་ན་ལྷག་མ་ཐམས་ཅད་འཆུག་འགྲོ་བ་བཞིན་དུ་ཀ་དག་གི་བཞུགས་ཚུལ་གྱི་གོ་དོན་འཆུག་ན་རྫོགས་པ་ཆེན་པོའི་ལམ་གྱི་ཁོག་རྟ་ཐམས་ཅད་འཆུག་འགྲོ་བ་ཡིན། ཀ་དག་དང་གདོད་མ་ཐོག་མ་སོགས་དོན་གཅིག་གི་གནད་ཀྱིས་ཡིན་པར་གསུང་། གཞན་ཡང་འཕྲོ་རྒོད་དང་བྱིང་རྨུག་གི་འབར་འབུར་དང་བྲལ་བ་མཉམ་ཡང་། དབང་ཤེས་དང་ཡིད་ཤེས་དེའི་བཙོན་པའི་རླུང་སོགས་གཤིས་ལ་མ་ཞུགས་པས་སེམས་ཀྱི་ཕྱོགས་སུ་གྱུར་

པ་ཐམས་ཅད་ཀྱིས་མི་ཚོགས་པས་ཟང་ཐལ། མར་མེ་བུམ་ནང་དུ་ཡོད་པ་བཞིན་དུ། ནང་གསལ་ལམ་གཏིང་གསལ་གཞོན་ནུ་བུམ་སྐུ་ཟེར། རིག་པ་དེ་གསལ་ངར་ཉི་མ་བརྒྱ་བས་ལྷག་པས་ན་རང་གསལ། བདེ་གསལ་མི་རྟོག་གསུམ་རང་ཆས་སུ་ཡོད་པས་ན་ལྷུན་གྲུབ། འདོད་སེམས་ལས་བསམ་གཏན་དང་པོ་ཕྲ། དང་པོ་ལས་གཉིས་པ་ཕྲ་བ་སོགས་རིམ་བཞིན་འོག་མ་ལས་གོང་མ་རྣམས་ཆེས་ཕྲ་བ་ཡིན་ལ། དེ་དག་ལས་ཀྱང་ཆེས་ཕྲ་བའི་ཤེས་པ་ཡིན་པས་ཆེས་ཕྲ་སྟེ། དེ་ཐམས་ཅད་ཀྱིས་འོད་གསལ་རིག་པའི་ཁྱད་ཆོས་མི་འདྲ་བ་རེ་དྲངས་ཏེ་སྟོན་རྒྱུ་ཡོད་པ་གོ་དགོས། དེ་ལྟ་བུའི་འོད་གསལ་གྱི་བཞུགས་ཚུལ་རང་གི་གོ་བའི་སྟེང་ནས་ངོ་འཕྲོད་དགོས། འོད་གསལ་ལ་དམར་འཛུས་བྱེད་ན་དྲན་པས་སྐྱོང་རྒྱུ་ཁོང་དུ་ཆུད་དགོས། འོད་གསལ་གྱི་བཞུགས་ཚུལ་བླ་མའི་མན་ངག་གིས་ངོ་སྤྲོད་པ་དེ་སེམས་ལས་མ་བོར་བར་ཡིད་ངོར་འདྲིས་ཐུབ་པ་ཞིག་དགོས། དེ་བོར་ན་ཁྲེགས་ཆོད་ཀྱི་ལམ་གྱི་སྲོག་སྟོར་བ་ཡིན། དེ་ནི་དཔེར་ན་བླ་མེད་རྒྱུད་སྡེ་གཞན་གྱི་རྩ་ཐིག་སོགས་ལ་གནད་དུ་བསྣུན་པ་དགོས་མེད་དུ་བཞག་ན་རྫོགས་རིམ་གྱི་སྲོག་སྟོར་བ་ཡིན་པ་དང་མཚུངས། དྭངས་སྙིགས་གཉིས་སུ་ཕྱེ་བའི་སེམས་ནི་སྙིགས་མ་དང་། རིག་པ་ནི་དྭངས་མའི་ཡང་ཞུན་བཅུད་དུ་དྲིལ་བ་ལྟ་བུ་ཡིན་ནོ། །མ་རིག་པའི་བག་ཆགས་ཟད་ནས་སངས་རྒྱས་ཀྱི་སྒྲུབ་བྱེད་རིག་པ་ཡིན། རིག་པ་ལམ་དུ་བྱས་ནས་སྐད་ཅིག་ཀྱང་འབྲལ་བ་མེད་པར་དྲན་པས་བསྐྱངས་ཏེ་བློ་ཤིན་ཏུ་རྒྱས་པར་བྱས་ནས་ཡོད་ན་རིག་པ་ལ་དམར་འཛུས་བྱེད་རྒྱུ་རླེད་ནས་རིག་པ་ངོ་འཕྲོད་པ་ཡིན། གློ་བུར་བའི་སེམས་ཀྱི་ངོ་བོ་སྐྱེ་མི་སྲིད་པ་དང་གནས་ལུགས་ལ་འགྱུར་བ་མེད་པས་ན་མ་བཅོས་པ་དང་། ཆོས་སྐུའི་རིག་པ། ཆོས་སྐུའི་བསྒྲུབ་གཞི་ཡིན་པ་ཤེས་དགོས། རྫོགས་ཆེན་ལ་རིག་པ་ཞེས་མིང་གི་ཐ་སྙད་འདོགས་པ་དེ་ནི་སྣང་

གསུམ་ལས་འདས་པའི་ཤེས་པ་སངས་རྒྱས་ཀྱི་བསྒྲུབ་གཞི་ཡིན་པས་རིག་པ་ཞེས་གསུངས་ལ། རིག་པའི་སྟེང་ན་མུན་པ་ཡོད་མ་མྱོང་བས་ན་འོད་གསལ་ཟེར། མ་རྒྱུད་ལས་བདེ་ཆེན་ལྷན་སྐྱེས་ཀྱི་ཡེ་ཤེས་ཟེར་བ་ནི་ཡེ་ནས་བདེ་ཆེན་དང་ཡེ་ཤེས་གཉིས་འབྲལ་མ་མྱོང་བར་ལྷན་སྐྱེས་ཀྱི་ཚུལ་དུ་ཡོད་པས་ན་ལྷན་སྐྱེས་ཀྱི་ཡེ་ཤེས་ཟེར། ཚེ་འདིའི་སྣང་སེམས་ཐམས་ཅད་ཕར་སྡུད་ས་ཚེ་ཕྱི་མའི་སྣང་སེམས་ཐམས་ཅད་ཚུར་མཆེད་སའི་སྤྱི་གཞི་འོད་གསལ་ཡིན། འོད་གསལ་ཉིད་ཀུན་རྟོག་དང་སེམས་ཀྱིས་ལྷེ་ཁ་བསྒྱུར་ནས་འགྲོ་མི་ཤེས་པས་ན་ཡེ་གྲོལ་འདུས་མ་བྱས་པ་ཞེས་བརྗོད། ངོ་རང་ཐོག་ཏུ་སྤྲད་པའི་ཚུལ་ནི། རང་ཐོག་ཅེས་པ་འོད་གསལ་རང་གི་ཐོག་ཏུ་སྤྲད་པ་ཡིན། ངོ་སྤྲོད་ཚུལ་ནི་གོང་སྨོས་བཞིན། བླ་མའི་མན་ངག་གིས་འོད་གསལ་གྱི་རྣམ་པའམ་བཞུགས་ཚུལ་ཇི་ལྟ་བ་བཞིན་བསྟན་ནས་སློབ་མ་ལ་གོ་བ་ཆགས་ངེས་ཅན་བྱེད་དགོས་པ་ཡིན། །ངོ་སྤྲོད་ཚུལ་གྱི་དཔེ་ནི། ནམ་མཁའ་སྤྲིན་འཐུག་གིས་བསྒྲིབ་སྐབས་ན་ནམ་མཁའི་ངོ་སྤྲད་ན་ངོ་འཕྲོད་པ་ཙུང་དཀའ་ལ། ནམ་མཁའི་ཕྱོགས་འགའ་ཞིག་ན་སྤྲིན་མེད་པའི་ནམ་མཁའ་ཙུང་ཟད་མཐོང་སར་ཕྱིན་ཏེ་ལྷོ་འཛམ་བུའི་གླིང་འདིའི་ནམ་མཁའ་ཐམས་ཅད་སྔོན་པོ་འདི་ལྟ་བུ་ཡིན་ཟེར་ནས་ངོ་སྤྲད་ན་ངོ་འཕྲོད་སླ་མོ་ཡོད། དེ་ལྟར་དུ་ད་ལྟ་ཀུན་རྟོག་དང་སེམས་ཀྱི་སྤྲིན་ཐག་སྤྲིན་འཁྲིགས་པ་ལྟ་བུའི་གནས་སྐབས་ན་འོད་གསལ་ངོ་སྤྲད་ན་ངོ་འཕྲོད་ཙུང་ཟད་དཀའ་སྟེ། འཆི་ཁ་དང་ཆོས་ཉིད་བར་དོའི་སྐབས་འོད་གསལ་འཆར་བ་དེ་ལྟར་དུ་ངོ་སྤྲད་ན་ངོ་འཕྲོད་པ་ཡིན། དེ་ནི་བླ་མས་འཆི་ཁ་དང་བར་དོའི་སྐབས་སུ་འོད་གསལ་འཆར་ཚུལ་སློབ་མ་ལ་ཞིབ་ཏུ་གསུངས་པ་ལྟར། སློབ་མ་རང་གི་གོ་བའི་སྟེང་ནས་མྱོང་བ་ཞིབ་མོ་ཆགས་དགོས། དེ་རྣམས་ངོ་རང་ཐོག་ཏུ་སྤྲད་པ་ཡིན། ཐག་གཅིག་ཐོག་ཏུ་བཅད་པ་ནི། འོད་གསལ་དེ་ནི་ད་

ལྷ་རང་གི་ཤེས་པ་འདིའི་ཕྱུག་ན་ཏིལ་ལ་སྣུམ་གྱིས་ཁྱབ་པ་བཞིན་དུ་སྐད་ཅིག་ཙམ་
ཡང་འབྲལ་མ་མྱོང་བར་ཡོད་ལ་བྲལ་ན་སངས་རྒྱས་ཡང་མི་འཚོ། སེམས་
ཅན་ཡང་མི་འཚོ། དེ་ཉིད་ཡོད་པ་ཐག་གཅིག་ཏུ་བཅད་ཐུབ་དགོས། དེ་
ལྟར་ཡོད་ནའང་འོད་གསལ་དེ་ཉིད་འཆི་དུས་མ་གཏོགས་ད་ལྟ་རང་ཉིད་ལ་འཆར་
བར་མི་འགྱུར་རམ་སྙམ་ན། མ་ཡིན་ཏེ་གཉིད་དུས་དང་བརྒྱལ་བ་ལ་སོགས་
པའི་སྐབས་སུ་ཡང་འཆར། ད་ལྟའི་སྐབས་སུ་འོད་གསལ་དེ་ཉིད་ངོ་སྤྲོད་པ་
ལྟར་དྲན་བྱ་དང་དྲན་བྱེད་འབེན་བཙུགས་པ་ལྟ་བུ་མ་ཡིན་པར། གང་ཟག་རང་
གིས་རང་དྲན་པ་བཞིན་དུ་དང་པོ་དྲན་པས་སེམས་ཀྱི་ཕྱོགས་ཐམས་ཅད་རྩིས་མེད་
དགོས་མེད་དུ་བཞག་ནས། རིག་པའི་ཕྱོགས་ཁོ་ན་ཡིད་ངོར་ཤར་བར་བྱས་
ནས་རིག་པའི་རང་བཞིན་མ་བཅོས་པར་བསྒོམ་དགོས། དྲན་པས་རིག་པའི་
རྣམ་པ་དེ་ཉིད་བོར་ན་སེམས་ཀྱི་ཐོག་ཏུ་ཐོན་པ་ཡིན། དཔེར་ན་ཁྱིམ་གྱི་གནས་
ཀྱི་ཁྲི་ཐོག་ནས་ལྷུང་ན་ཁྱིམ་ལས་འདའ་བ་མེད་པའི་དཔེ་དེ་བཞིན་དུ་རིག་པ་དེ་
ཉིད་དྲན་པས་བོར་སོང་ན་སེམས་ལས་འདའ་བ་མེད་པ་ཡིན། སེམས་སལ་
ལེ་ཧྲིག་གེ་བ་བསྒོམ་ན་རིག་པ་བསྒོམ་པའི་གོ་མི་ཆོད་པ་ཡིན། ཡང་དཔེ་
གཅིག་ནི་བཞི་ཆ་གསུམ་བྲལ་ཏེ། གསུམ་དང་བྲལ་བའི་བཞི་པའི་ཆ་ནི་རིག་
པ་ཞེས་བརྗོད་ཚོག་སྟེ། དེའི་རྒྱུ་མཚན་སེམས་ཀྱི་ཆ་གཅིག་རིག་པ་ཡིན་པའི་
གནད་ཀྱིས་རིག་པ་ཞེས་བཏགས་ན་ཆོག །གསུམ་དང་བྲལ་བའི་བཞི་ཆའི་
སྐབས་ན་རིག་པ་ངོ་སྤྲོད་ན་འཕྲོད་སླ་བ་ཡིན་གསུང་། དེའི་སྐབས་ན་ལྷ་བཟོའི་
ཚོན་གྱིས་སྐུ་རིས་བྱེད་པ་དང་འདྲ་བ་ཡིན་གསུང་། དྲན་པས་རིག་པ་བསྐྱངས་
པའི་གནས་སྐབས་ན་རིག་པ་མངོན་དུ་གྱུར་ཡོད་ཨེ་དགོས་སྙམ་ན་མི་དགོས་ཏེ།
དཔེར་ན་ཁང་པའི་ནང་ཞིག་ན་མི་གྲལ་གང་ཡོད་སྐབས་ན། དེའི་གྲལ་གྱི་མི་
གཅིག་ལ་དམིགས་ནས་སྟོད་པའི་སྐབས་མི་གཞན་རྣམས་ལ་ཅང་མི་སེམས་པར་

གྱུར་ཏེ་མི་གཞན་རྣམས་རིམ་པ་བཞིན་དུ་མི་གཅིག་ལ་ཐིམ་སོང་བ་ཡང་མ་ཡིན། དེ་རྣམས་ལ་སེམས་ཀྱི་ཟུར་གྱིས་བལྟས་ནས་སྤྱོད་པ་ཡང་མ་ཡིན། མི་དེ་རྣམས་ལ་ཅི་ཡང་མི་སེམས་པ་བཞིན་དུ་དྲན་པས་རིག་པ་ལ་བལྟས་ནས་བསྒོམ་པའི་སྐབས་དྲན་པ་རིག་པ་ལ་འདྲེས་སོང་ལྟ་བུར་འབྱུང་མོད། འདྲེས་སོང་སྙམ་པའི་མོས་པ་བྱེད་མི་དགོས། ད་ལྟ་རང་ལ་འོད་གསལ་འཆར་ཡོད་པ་ཡང་བསམ་མི་དགོས། དཔེར་ན་སངས་རྒྱས་མཚན་བཟང་པོས་བརྒྱན་པ་ཞིག་སྒོམ་ནས་སངས་རྒྱས་ཀྱི་རྣམ་པ་ཡིད་ལ་ཤར་ཡོད་པའི་དུས་ན་ངའི་སངས་རྒྱས་བསྒོམ་ཡོད་བསམ་མི་དགོས། སངས་རྒྱས་ཡིད་ལ་སྒོམ་ཡོད་པའི་ཕྱིར་རོ། །དེ་བཞིན་དུ་ང་ལ་འོད་གསལ་ཤར་ཡོད་བསམ་དགོས་པ་མ་ཡིན་ཏེ། སྔར་བླ་མས་ངོ་སྤྲོད་པའི་འོད་གསལ་དེ་ཉིད་རང་གིས་སྒོམ་བཞིན་པའི་དུས་ཡིན་པས་སོ། །ཨོ་རྒྱན་རིན་པོ་ཆེའི་ཞལ་ནས། ཕྱི་ལྟར་གཟུང་བའི་སོགས་ལྟར་འོད་གསལ་རང་ངོ་ཤེས་པ་སྟེ། བླ་མའི་མན་ངག་གིས་རིག་པ་ངོ་སྤྲོད་པ་དེ་ལ་དྲན་པས་རིག་པ་བསྐྱངས་ནས་འདུག་ན་བར་དུ་འོད་གསལ་རང་ངོ་ཤེས་ནས་ཕྱི་ལྟར་གཟུང་བའི་ཡུལ་སྣང་རྣམས་རང་ཤུགས་ཀྱིས་དག་འགྲོ་བ་ཡིན། དྲན་པ་དང་རིག་པ་བསྲེས་ནས་སྒོམ་བསྡད་ན་ནང་དུ་འཛིན་པའི་སེམས་རྣམས་རིག་པ་ལ་ཐིམ་པའམ་རང་བཞིན་གྱིས་དྭངས་འགྲོ་བ་ཡིན། དེ་བཞིན་དུ་རིག་པ་དྲན་པས་མ་བརྗེད་པར་སྐྱོང་ནས་སྡོད་ན་བར་དུ་འོད་གསལ་རང་ངོ་ཤེས་ནས་འགྲོ་ངེས་པ་ཡིན་གསུང་། རིག་པ་དེ་ཉིད་བསྐྱང་བསྡད་ན་རླན་གར་ཡོད་སར་ཆུ་འགྲོ་བ་བཞིན་དུ། རིག་པའི་རྩལ་ལས་སེམས་རྣམས་འཕྲོས་པ་ཡིན་པས། མཐར་སེམས་རྣམས་རིག་པ་རང་ཉིད་ལ་ཐིམ་ནས་འགྲོ་བ་ཡིན་ཏེ། རིག་པ་རང་གི་ཚང་ངམ་མལ་གྱི་ལམ་ཀླེད་འོང་བ་ཡིན། དཔེར་ན་རྒྱ་མཚོའི་རྦ་རླབས་རྒྱ་མཚོ་ལས་བྱུང་ནས་མཐར་རྒྱ་མཚོ་ལ་ཐིམ་འགྲོ་བ་བཞིན་དུ་རིག་པའི་

རྩལ་གྱི་སེམས་རྣམས་རིག་པ་ལས་འཕྲོ་ཞིང་མཐར་ལམ་བསྒོམ་སྟོབས་ཀྱིས་རྩལ་རྣམས་རིག་པ་རང་ཉིད་ལ་ཐིམ་པའམ་རིག་པའི་དབྱིངས་སུ་དྭངས་ནས་འགྲོ་བ་ཡིན་པས་དེའི་ཚེ་འགྱུ་བ་རང་དག་གི་དགོངས་པ་ཞེས་བརྗོད་དོ། །དབང་པོའི་སྒོ་སྡོམ་པ་ཡང་། བསྐྱེད་རིམ་དུ་ནི་རྗེས་ཐོབ་ཏུ་སྣོད་བཅུད་དག་པ་རབ་འབྱམས་ལྷའི་དཀྱིལ་འཁོར་དུ་བལྟ་བ་དང་། རྫོགས་རིམ་དུ་གང་སྣང་བ་བདེ་ཆེན་གྱི་རྣམ་རོལ་དུ་ལྟ་བ་དང་། སྐབས་འདིར་གང་སྣང་རིག་པའི་རྩལ་ལམ། གང་སྣང་རིག་པའི་རྣམ་འཕྲུལ་དུ་དྭངས་གསལ་བདེ་བའི་རྣམ་པར་རྩལ་སྦྱོང་བ་དེའོ། །མདོར་ན་སེམས་དང་རིག་པ་གཉིས་ཀྱི་སྤང་བླང་ཕྱེས་ནས་དྲན་པས་རིག་པའི་བཞུགས་ཚུལ་སྐྱོང་དགོས། དེ་ལྟར་སྐྱོང་བ་ལ་ཡང་དང་པོ་རྩོལ་བའི་དྲན་པས་རིག་པ་དང་བསྲེས་ནས་བསྒོམ་དགོས། མཐར་འདུ་བྱེད་ཀྱི་དྲན་པ་རྣམས་རང་དག་ལ་སོང་ནས་རིག་པའི་རང་མདངས་ཁོང་ནས་འཆར་ཡོང་། དེའི་སྐབས་སུ་རྩོལ་མེད་རང་བཞག་གི་དྲན་པ་ཞེས་ཟེར་རོ། །ཡེ་གྲོལ་འདུས་མ་བྱས་ཀྱི་རིག་པ་དེ་རང་གི་ཤེས་པའི་ཆ་ན་ཡོད་པ་བླ་མའི་མན་ངག་གིས་ངོ་སྤྲོད་ནས་ཐག་ཆོད་པ་ཞིག་ངེས་པར་དགོས་ཞེས་ཡང་ནས་ཡང་དུ་ནན་ཆེ་བར་གསུངས་པས། འདིར་ཡང་བློས་སྐྱོན་ལ་མ་བསམ་པར་གསུང་རིམ་ལྟར་བརྗེད་བྱང་དུ་བྱས་པ་ཡིན། དེ་ལྟ་བུའི་འོད་གསལ་རིག་པ་དེ་ཉིད་རྫོགས་ཆེན་གྱི་རྒྱུད་ནས་གཏན་ལ་ཕབ་ཚུལ། རྡོ་རྗེའི་གད་མོ་བཅུ་གཉིས། ཚིག་ཆེན་པོ་བརྒྱད། བཞག་ཐབས་རྣམ་པ་བདུན། ཅོག་བཞག་རྣམ་པ་བཞི་ལ་སོགས་པའི་སྒོ་ནས་གཏན་ལ་ཕབ་ཚུལ་མང་དུ་གསུངས་ཀྱང་། མདོར་ན་སྐབས་འདིར་བསྟན་པའི་ཚིག་གསུམ་གནད་དུ་བསྡུ་བའི་ཁོངས་སུ་དེ་ཐམས་ཅད་ཚིག་གི་ཆ་ནས་མ་འདུ་ན་ཡང་དོན་གྱི་ཆ་ནས་འདུ་བ་ཡིན། རྡོ་རྗེའི་གད་མོ་བཅུ་གཉིས་ཀྱི་ནང་ནས། རྫོགས་པ་ཆེན་པོ་ནི་རྒྱུ་འབྲས་ལས་འདས་པའི་ཆོས་

ཡིན་ཏ་ཏ། ཞེས་བརྗོད་པའི་དོན་ནི། ཐེག་པ་གཞན་གྱི་རྒྱུ་འབྲས་ལ་སྐུར་བ་བཏབ་པ་མིན་ཏེ། རྒྱུ་འབྲས་གཉིས་ཀ་སྣང་གསུམ་ཚུན་ཆད་ཀྱི་སེམས་ཀྱི་སྟེང་ན་ཡོད་པས་སོ། །རྫོགས་པ་ཆེན་པོའི་གཞིས་དེར་ཕེབས་པ་རྣམས་ལ་མཚམས་མེད་པ་ལྔ་བྱས་པ་དང་བསྐལ་པ་མང་པོ་ཚོགས་བསགས་པ་གཉིས་སངས་རྒྱས་པར་ཁྱད་མེད་གསུངས་པ་ནི། ཡེ་གྲོལ་འདུས་མ་བྱས་ཀྱི་རིག་པ་ལ་དགོངས་ནས་གསུངས་པ་ཡིན་...འདི་ལྟ་བུ་ལ་དགེ་སྡིག་གིས་མི་གོས་པ་སྒྲ་དྲང་ཐད་རང་དུ་བསྟན་པ་ཡིན་ལ། གཞིས་དེར་མ་ཕེབས་པ་དག་ལ་དེ་ལྟར་བསྟན་པའམ་ཆཤད་པ་མིན་ནོ། །མཆན།ལ་མཚན་གཞི་གཞིས་དེར་ཕེབས་པའི་རྣལ་འབྱོར་པ་ཏེ་ལོ་པ་དང་བི་མ་ལ་ལྟ་བུའོ། །ཀུན་ཏུ་བཟང་པོ་ཉིད་ཀྱིས་ཀྱང་དགེ་བ་ཙུང་ཟད་མ་བྱས་སྡིག་པ་ཙུང་ཟད་ཙམ་ཡང་མ་སྤྱངས་ནས་སངས་རྒྱས་སོ་ཞེས། དགེ་སྡིག་ལས་འདས་པར་གསུངས་པ་ཡང་། འོད་གསལ་ཉག་གཅིག་ལ་དགོངས་ཏེ་གསུངས་པ་ཡིན་ལ། དེའི་རྒྱུ་མཚན་ནི་འོད་གསལ་ཉིད་ནི་དམྱལ་བའི་མེ་དང་གྲང་བའི་ངད་དང་ཡི་དྭགས་སུ་བཀྲེས་སྐོམ་གྱི་སྡུག་བསྔལ་སོགས་ཐམས་ཅད་ཀྱིས་གོས་མ་མྱོང་ལ་འོད་གསལ་དེ་ཉིད་སྡུག་བསྔལ་གྱི་ངོ་བོར་སྐྱེ་མི་སྲིད་པས་དེ་ཉིད་སྒྲ་དྲང་ཐད་དུ་གསུངས་པ་ཡིན། མདོར་ན་སྣང་མཆེད་ཐོབ་གསུམ་གྱི་སྔོན་གྱི་སྣང་སེམས་རགས་པའི་སྟེང་ནས་རྒྱུ་བསགས་ནས་འབྲས་བུ་མྱོང་བ་སོགས་འཇོག་པ་ཡིན་པ་གལ་ཆེ། ཀུན་བཟང་དགེ་བ་རྡུལ་ཙམ་མ་བྱས་པར། །ཟག་མེད་རང་ངོ་ཤེས་པའི་དགེ་ཚོགས་ཀྱིས། །ཞེས་གསུངས་པ་ལྟར་རོ། །ཕྱི་འདུ་འཛི་ལས་ལོ་བརྒྱུར་བསྒྲུབས་པ་ལས་རི་ཁྲོད་དབེན་པར་གཅིག་པུར་གནས་ནས་ཉིན་གཅིག་དགེ་བ་བསྒྲུབ་པ་ཁེབས་ཆེ་བ་དང་། རང་གི་སེམས་གཙང་སེང་ངེ་བ་ཡིན་པས། དེ་ཕྱི་རི་ཁྲོད་ཀྱི་དབེན་པ་ཡིན་ནོ། །ནང་རྣམ་རྟོག་ལས་དབེན་པ་ནི། སྤྱིར་ན་ཕར་ཕྱིན་ཐེག་པའི་ཞི་ལྷག་གྲུབ་ནས་

སེམས་བཏང་འགྲོ་བཞག་སྤྱོད་ལ་རང་དབང་བའི་ལུས་སེམས་ལས་སུ་རུང་བས་གང་ལ་དམིགས་ཀྱང་དགེ་བ་ལ་བཀོལ་དུ་རུང་བ་ཡིན་ནོ། །རྣམ་རྟོག་སྤྲུན་ཐག་ཆད་པའི་ནམ་མཁའ་ལྟ་བུའི་འོད་གསལ་ནི་གསང་བའི་རི་ཁྲོད་དུ་འཛོག་ཏེ། འོད་གསལ་དེ་ལ་ལྟོས་ན་སེམས་བཏང་འགྲོ་བཞག་སྤྱོད་ལ་དབང་བའི་རྣམ་པ་དེ་ཡང་སྐབས་ཞད་ཅན་ཞིག་ཡིན་པར་གསུངས་ལ། དེ་གསང་བ་སེམས་ཀྱིས་དབེན་པའི་རི་ཁྲོད་ཡིན། །དེ་ལྟར་ལམ་གྱི་མྱུར་བུལ་ཡང་ཕར་ཕྱིན་ཐེག་པའི་ཟབ་རྒྱས་གཉིས་ལྡན་གྱི་ལམ་བསྐལ་པ་གྲངས་མེད་མང་པོར་བསྒྲུབས་ནས་མཐར་མངོན་པར་རྫོགས་པར་སངས་རྒྱས་པ་ཡིན་ལ། སྔགས་ཀྱི་ལམ་ནི་དེ་ལས་ཤིན་ཏུ་མྱུར་སྟེ་ཕྱི་རྒྱུད་སྡེ་གསུམ་གྱི་ལམ་གྱིས་ཐུན་མོང་གི་དངོས་གྲུབ་སོགས་བསྒྲུབས་ནས། དེ་ལས་ཚེ་བསྐལ་པ་མང་པོར་བསྲིང་ནས་ད་གཟོད་མཆོག་གི་དངོས་གྲུབ་ཐོབ་པ་ཡིན་གསུང་། བླ་མེད་ཀྱི་རྒྱུད་སྡེ་གཞན་གྱི་ལམ་ལ་ཚེ་བསྲིང་མི་དགོས་པར་མི་ལོ་བཅུ་གཉིས་ཀྱིས་མཆོག་གི་དངོས་གྲུབ་ཐོབ། ཐེག་དགུའི་ཡང་རྩེ་འདི་ཉིད་ཀྱི་ལམ་གྱིས་མི་ལོ་དྲུག་གིས་མཆོག་གི་དངོས་གྲུབ་ཐོབ་སྟེ་མྱུར་བུལ་གྱི་ཁྱད་པར་ཡང་དེ་ལྟ་བུ་ཡིན་ནོ། །མདོར་ན་ཀ་དག་ཁྲེགས་ཆོད་ཀྱི་རིག་པའི་བཞུགས་ཚུལ་དེ་ཉིད་འཆི་སྲིད་ཀྱི་འོད་གསལ་ཇི་ལྟ་བ་བཞིན་དུ་ངོ་སྤྲོད་ནས། དེའི་ཁྱད་ཆོས་ཀ་དག་ཟང་ཐལ་ལ་སོགས་པའི་བརྗོད་ཚུལ་སྣ་ཚོགས་པའི་སྒོ་ནས་ཡོན་ཏན་གྱི་ཆ་མི་འདྲ་བ་རེ་རེ་བསྟན་ནས་རིག་པའི་བཞུགས་ཚུལ་ཇི་ལྟ་བ་བཞིན་བླ་མའི་མན་ངག་གིས་ངོ་ལེགས་པར་སྤྲོད་དེ་ད་ལྟ་རང་གི་དྲན་པ་ལ་ལེགས་པར་འདྲིས་ངེས་སུ་བྱེད། དེ་འདྲ་བའི་རིག་པ་དེ་དོན་གཞན་དུ་ཡོད་པ་མ་ཡིན་ཏེ། དེ་ལྟའི་རང་གི་ཤེས་པ་འདི་ཉིད་ཀྱི་ཆ་ཞད་མ་ཐག་པ་དེ་ཉིད་ཡིན་པར་ཐག་བཅད་ནས་བཅད་ཐོག་དེ་ནས་རིག་པའི་རྣམ་པ་དེ་ཉིད་དྲན་པས་སྐད་ཅིག་ཀྱང་མི་བརྗེད་པར་བདག་གི་སེམས་འདི་ཉིད། རིག་པའི་ངོ་

བོར་གྱུར་སོང་སླམ་པ་ལྟ་བུའི་མོས་སྒོམ་ཡང་མ་ཡིན་པར་ད་ལྟའི་རང་གི་ཤེས་པའི་ཆ་འདི་དག་ཐམས་ཅད་རིག་པའི་རང་བཞིན་དུ་བལྟས་ནས་སེམས་ཀྱི་ཕྱོགས་ལ་ཅུང་ཟད་ཙམ་ཡང་མི་གཡེང་བར་རིག་པའི་ཕྱོགས་ལེགས་པར་བསྒོམ་པར་བྱ་བ་ནི་གནད་དོན་ཐུན་མོང་མ་ཡིན་པ་ཡིན་ནོ། །དེས་ཐག་གཅིག་ཐོག་ཏུ་བཅད་པ་སོང་། གསུམ་པ་གདེང་གྲོལ་ཐོག་ཏུ་བཅའ་བ་ནི། སྒོམ་པ་རབ་དང་། འབྲིང་དང་། ཐ་མ་གསུམ་ལས། བསྒོམ་པ་རབ་སེང་གེ་ལ་རྡོ་འཕང་བ་ལྟ་བུ་ཡིན་ཏེ། སེང་གེ་ལ་རྡོ་ལ་འཕངས་ཀྱང་རྡོ་རྗུར་མི་འདེད་པར་རྡོ་འཕང་མཁན་པོ་རང་དེད་ནས་ཉེས་ལན་གྱི་ཆད་པ་གཅོད་ནས་རྡོ་དེ་སླར་མི་ཕོག་པར་བྱེད་པ་ལྟར། སྒོམ་རབ་ཀྱིས་རྣམ་རྟོག་ཐོལ་གྱིས་སྐྱེས་ཚེ་རྣམ་རྟོག་གི་རྗེས་སུ་མི་འབྲང་ཞིང་རྣམ་རྟོག་འཆར་མཁན་པོ་རང་དྲན་པས་ཧད་ཀྱིས་བཟུང་ནས་རྣམ་རྟོག་གང་ཤར་རྣམས་རང་གྲོལ་དུ་གཏོང་བའོ། །འགའ་ཞིག་གིས་དེའི་སྐབས་རྣམ་རྟོག་ལ་ཅེར་རེ་ལྟོས་ཞེས་པའི་དོན་དེ་རྣམ་རྟོག་ཁོ་རང་ལ་བལྟ་བ་ཡང་ཡོད། འགའ་ཞིག་གིས་རྣམ་རྟོག་སྔ་ཕྱིའི་བར་སེམས་སལ་ལེ་ཧྲིག་གེ་བ་ལ་བལྟ་བ་ཡང་ཡོད། དེ་གཉིས་གང་ཡང་མ་ཡིན་པར་རང་ལུགས་ལ་ཅེ་རེ་ལྟོས་ཞེས་པའི་དོན་ནི། རིག་པ་ཁོ་རང་ལ་བལྟ་བ་ཡིན་ལ། རིག་པ་ལ་བལྟ་བ་དེའི་སྐབས་སེམས་ཀྱི་ཕྱོགས་ལ་དྲན་པས་བདག་ཅུང་ཟད་ཙམ་ཡང་མི་བྱེད་པ་ནི་སྐབས་འདིའི་གནད་དོན་གཅིག་གོ། །སྒོམ་པ་ཐ་མ་ནི་ཁྱི་ལ་རྡོ་འཕངས་པ་ལྟར་རྡོ་འཕེན་པ་པོ་དེ་བསྐྱུར་ནས་རྡོ་རྗུ་དེད་པ་ལྟར། དེ་བཞིན་དུ་རྣམ་རྟོག་ཤར་མཁན་བསྐྱུར་ཏེ། སྒོམ་རྣམ་རྟོག་གི་རྗུར་དེད་པ་དེ་འདྲ་མིན་པར་ཤར་མཁན་པོ་རང་ལ་བལྟ་བ་དེ་ཡིན། གྲོལ་ལུགས་གསུམ་ནི། རྣམ་རྟོག་ངོ་ཤེས་པ་སྔར་འདྲིས་ཀྱི་མི་དང་འཕྲད་པ་ལྟ་བུ། རིག་པའི་རྣམ་པ་བརྗོད་ན་ཇི་ཞིག་ན་རྣམ་རྟོག་ཤར་ཡོང་བ་དེ་ངོ་ཤེས་ནས་དེ་ལ་སྐྱོན་དུ་བལྟས་ནས་སྔར་གྱི་

རིག་པའི་བཞུགས་ཚུལ་གྱི་སྟེང་དུ་འཛོག་པ་དེའོ། །ཉམས་རྟོག་རང་གིས་རང་
གྲོལ་བ་སྦྲུལ་གྱི་མདུད་པ་ཞིག་པ་ལྟ་བུའི་གྲོལ་ཚུལ་ནི། འོད་གསལ་གྱི་ཉམས་
པ་དེ་ཉིད་ཀྱི་བཞུགས་ཚུལ་ལམ་དུ་བྱེད་དུས་ཉམས་རྟོག་གཞན་གྱིས་བར་གཅོད་མི་
ནུས་ནའང་། དྲན་པས་རིག་པ་ཙུང་ཟད་བསྒྲིམས་ནས་མ་བསྐྱུང་ན་ཡེངས་
ནས་འགྲོ་ཉེན་ཡོད་པས་ཙུང་ཟད་བསྒྲིམས་པའི་སྟོབས་ཀྱིས་ཉམས་རྟོག་གི་ཚུགས་
མི་ཐུབ་པར་རང་སར་གྲོལ་བ་དེའོ། །གསུམ་པ་ཉམས་རྟོག་ཕན་མེད་གནོད་མེད་
དུ་གྲོལ་ཚུལ་ཁང་སྟོང་ནང་དུ་རྐུན་མ་བྱུང་ན་རྐུན་མ་ལ་ཐོབ་པ་དང་ཁང་པའི་ནང་
གྱི་རྒྱུ་རྫས་ལ་ཤར་བ་མེད་པ་ལྟར། དེའི་དུས་སུ་དྲན་པས་རིག་པའི་མཁར་
ཚུགས་ནས། ཐ་མལ་གྱི་ཉམས་རྟོག་ཐལ་ཐོལ་རེ་སྐྱེས་ན་ཡང་། ཉམས་རྟོག
ལ་ཐོབ་རྒྱུ་དང་འོད་གསལ་ལ་འཚོར་རྒྱུ་མེད་པ་དེའོ། །མདོར་ན་དྲན་པའི་
མདུང་དེ་ཉིད་རིག་པའི་གཏིང་དུ་བཙུགས་ནས་གཞན་རྐྱེན་གྱིས་བཟི་མི་ནུས་པ་
དགོས་ཏེ། ཆུའི་ཁར་ཙམ་སྐྱུ་གཏོར་བ་ལྟ་བུར་ཡར་མར་དུ་ཡ་ལ་ལ་བྱེད་པ་ལྟ་
བུ་ནི་མ་ཡིན་ནོ། །དེ་ནས་རིམ་པ་བཞིན་འཇུར་དྲན་གྱི་དྲན་པའམ་འདུ་བྱེད་ཀྱི་
དྲན་པ་ཧ་ཟད་དུ་སོང་ནས། འོད་གསལ་རང་གི་ངོས་ནས་དྲན་པ་ཞིག་སད་
ཆས་སད་ཆས་བྱེད་པ་ཡིན་ཏེ། དེ་སད་ནས་རིག་པ་རང་ལ་ཡོད་པའི་དྲན་པ་
ཁྱད་པར་བ་ཞིག་འབྱུང་ལ། དེ་ལ་རྩོལ་མེད་རང་བཞག་གི་དྲན་པ་ཞེས་བརྗོད་
དོ། །རིག་པའི་རྩལ་སྣང་བ་ནི་མཉམ་བཞག་གི་སྐབས་རིག་པ་ལ་མཉམ་པར་
བཞག་པའི་སྟོབས་ཀྱིས་རྗེས་ཐོབ་ཀྱི་སྣང་བ་ཐམས་ཅད་དྭངས་གསལ་བདེ་བའི་
ཉམས་པར་འཆར་སྟེ། དཔེར་ན་མི་ཞིག་གིས་ཡིད་འོང་གི་བུམ་པ་མཐོང་བའི་
དཔེ་དེ་བཞིན་དུ་མཉམ་བཞག་གི་གནས་སྐབས་སུ་རིག་པའི་བཞུགས་ཚུལ་གྱི་
ཉམས་པ་ལས་སེམས་གཞན་དུ་མ་ཡེངས་པའི་སྟོབས་ཀྱིས་རྗེས་ཐོབ་ཏུ་ཡུལ་སྣང་
ཐམས་ཅད་དྭངས་གསལ་བདེ་བའི་ཉམས་པ་ཅན་དུ་འཆར་ཏེ། དེ་ལྟར་འཆར་

བའི་གང་ཟག་དེས་གང་སྣང་ཐམས་ཅད་རིག་པའི་རྣམ་འཕྲུལ་དུ་འཆར་ཐུབ་ལ། དེ་ཐུབ་ན་དེ་འདྲའི་སྟུགས་པ་དེས་ཕྱི་ནང་གི་སྣོད་བཅུད་ཐམས་ཅད་ཀྱང་རིག་པའི་རྣམ་འཕྲུལ་དུ་འཛོག་ཐུབ་པ་ཡིན་ནོ། །རྒྱུ་མཚན་དེས་ན་སྣོད་བཅུད་ཐམས་ཅད་རང་ངོས་ནས་མ་གྲུབ་པའི་གནད་ཀྱིས་རྣལ་འབྱོར་པས་ལམ་བསྒོམས་སྟོབས་ཀྱི་རིག་པའི་རྣམ་འཕྲུལ་དུ་འཛོག་ཐུབ་པས་སྣོད་བཅུད་གཉིས་བདེན་མེད་དུ་གཏན་ལ་ཕབ་ནུས་པ་ཡིན་ནོ། །དེ་ཡང་དང་པོ་ནས་བྱུང་གནས་འགྲོ་གསུམ་གྱི་སྐབས་སུ་སེམས་གཞི་མེད་རྩ་བྲལ་དུ་གཏན་ལ་ཕབ་དགོས་ཏེ། རིག་པའི་རྣམ་པ་ལམ་བྱེད་བསྒོམ་པའི་མཉམ་བཞག་དེ་ལས་ལྡང་བའི་རྗེས་ཐོབ་ཏུ་རིག་པའི་རྩལ་སྦྱངས་པའི་སྒོ་ནས་ཡུལ་སྣང་བདེན་མེད་དུ་གཏན་ལ་ཕབ་པའི་སྐབས་ཡིན་པས་སོ། །དེ་ལྟར་དང་པོ་སྟོང་པ་ཉིད་ལ་བློ་སྦྱང་བར་བྱས་ནས་གཞི་གྲོལ་ཀ་དག་གི་རིག་པ་ལ་མཉམ་པར་བཞག་པའི་སྐབས་སུ་རིག་པའི་བཞུགས་ཚུལ་ཁོ་ན་མ་གཏོགས་སྟོང་ཉིད་སོགས་ལ་དཔྱད་པ་བྱས་ནས་རིག་པའི་མལ་ས་འཁྲུག་པར་མི་བྱེད་པ་ཡང་གནད་དོ། །རིག་པ་མངོན་དུ་གྱུར་ཙམ་ཁྲིགས་ཆོད་ཀྱི་སྐབས་སུ་དབྱིངས་རིག་བསྲེ་དགོས་ཏེ། དེ་ནི་རིག་པའི་ངོ་བོ་རང་བཞིན་གྱིས་མ་གྲུབ་པའི་སྟོང་ཉིད་དམ་དབྱིངས་གཉིས་དོན་གཅིག་སྟེ། སྟོང་པའི་རང་མདངས་གསལ་ལ་འགགས་པ་མེད་པའི་རང་བཞིན་ཅན་དེ་ཉིད་རིག་པ་ཡིན་ལ། དེ་དང་དེའི་དབྱིངས་སྟོང་ཉིད་གཉིས་བསྲེས་ནས་བསྒོམ་ན་ནི་དབྱིངས་རིག་བསྲེས་པ་ཡིན་ཏེ། དེ་ནི་ཕར་ཕྱིན་ཐེག་པའི་ལམ་གྱིས་སྟོང་ཉིད་ལ་ཅི་ཙམ་གོམས་པར་བྱས་ཀྱང་ཟབ་ལམ་འདི་ཉིད་ཀྱིས་དབྱིངས་རིག་བསྲེས་ནས་བསྒོམ་པ་ནི་སྔ་མ་ལ་ལྟོས་ན་འགྲན་ཟླ་དང་བྲལ་བ་ཡིན་ལ། དེ་ནི་ཡུལ་སྣང་སྟོང་ཉིད་ལ་བཟང་ངན་མེད་ཀྱང་ཡུལ་ཅན་གྱི་རིག་པའམ་བསྒྲུབ་གཞིའི་ཁྱད་པར་ལས་ཡིན་པ་ཞེས་དགོས། དེ་འདྲའི་ལམ་ཟབ་མོ་འདི་ཉིད་རང་ཁོ་ན་ཞི་བདེ་དོན་དུ་གཉེར་

ནས་ཉམས་སུ་ལེན་པར་འདོད་པ་ནི། ཙྃཎྜན་ས་མཆོག་སོལ་བར་བྱེད་པ་དང་
འདྲ་གསུངས་ཏེ། རང་ཁོ་ནའི་དོན་དུ་གཉེར་བ་ཙམ་ཞིག་ནི་ཐེག་མཆོག
རྫོགས་པ་ཆེན་པོའི་ལམ་མིན་ཏེ། ངེས་འབྱུང་གི་བསམ་པ་དང་ལྡན་པས་སྟོང་
ཉིད་ཁོ་ན་བསྒོམ་པར་བྱེད་ན་ཐར་པ་ཙམ་ཞིག་ནི་ཐོབ་ནུས་ལ། དེ་ཙམ་ཞིག
གིས་ནི་ཆོག་པ་མིན་ཏེ། སེམས་ཅན་ཐམས་ཅད་ཀྱི་སྡུག་བསྔལ་རྒྱ་ཆོད
གཅིག་གི་ཡུན་ལའང་མི་བཟོད་པའི་སེམས་ཀྱིས་ཀུན་ནས་བསླངས་ཏེ།
སྙིགས་དུས་ཀྱི་ཚེ་ཐུང་ངུ་གཅིག་ལ་སངས་རྒྱས་ཀྱི་གོ་འཕང་དུས་མྱུར་བ་ཉིད་དུ
ཐོབ་པའི་ཆེད་དུ་རྫོགས་པ་ཆེན་པོའི་གདམས་ངག་ཉན་ནས་ཉམས་སུ་ལེན་པ་ཞིག
དགོས་སོ། །མདོ་སྔགས་གང་ཡིན་ཀྱང་བསྒྲུབ་བྱ་ཆོས་གཟུགས་ཀྱི་སྐུ་གཉིས
ལ་ཁྱད་པར་མེད་ཀྱང་། སྒྲུབ་བྱེད་ཀྱི་ལམ་ལ་ཁྱད་པར་འོད་པ་ཡིན་ཏེ། དེ
རྣམས་མདོར་བསྡུས་ནས་འདིར་སྐབས་སུ་བབས་པའི་རྣམ་བཞག་ཙུང་ཟད་བརྗོད
ན། བླ་མེད་ཀྱི་རྒྱུད་སྡེ་གཞན་གྱི་ལམ་རྩ་ཐིག་རླུང་སོགས་ལ་བསྟེན་ནས
གནད་དུ་བསྣུན་སྟོབས་ཀྱིས་སློང་བྱེད་ཀྱི་རྐྱེན་གསུམ་དང་བྲལ་བའི་ནམ་མཁའ
ལྟ་བུའི་བདེ་བ་ཆེན་པོའི་ཡེ་ཤེས་མངོན་དུ་བྱས་ནས་ཡེ་ཤེས་ཆོས་སྐུ་ཉིད་སྒྲུབ་པ
དང་། རིག་པ་དེ་ལས་ཙུང་ཟད་གཡོ་བར་རྩོམ་པ་དང་འོད་གསལ་གྱི་ལྷན་ཅིག
བྱེད་རྐྱེན་དང་རླུང་འོད་ཟེར་ལྔ་པའི་ཉེར་ལེན་གྱི་རྒྱུ་བྱས་ནས་རྟེན་དང་བརྟེན་པ
ལྷའི་དཀྱིལ་འཁོར་གྱི་རྣམ་པར་ལྡང་ནས་སངས་རྒྱས་ཀྱི་གཟུགས་སྐུ་སྒྲུབ་པ
དང་། འོད་གསལ་རྫོགས་པ་ཆེན་པོའི་ལམ་གྱིས་ཆོས་གཟུགས་ཀྱི་སྐུ་གཉིས
མངོན་དུ་བྱེད་ཚུལ་ནི། ཐུར་ངོ་སྤྲད་པའི་གཞི་དུས་ཀྱི་རིག་པ་དེ་ཉིད་ངོ་མཚར
བའི་ཆོས་དྲུ་མ་དང་བཅས་པའི་སྒོ་ནས་གཏན་ལ་ཕབ་ནས་རིག་པའི་བཞུགས
ཚུལ་ཇི་ལྟ་བ་བཞིན་དུ་བསྒོམས་ནས་ཡེ་ཤེས་ཆོས་ཀྱི་སྐུ་སྒྲུབ་པ་དང་། དེ་ལྟ
བུའི་གཞི་དུས་ཀྱི་འོད་གསལ་དེར་སྣང་བ་སྣ་ཚོགས་དང་དྲན་རིག་སྣ་ཚོགས

བསྐྱེད་པའི་ནུས་པ་ཡོད་ཀྱང་མ་སད་པའི་གནས་སྐབས་ཡིན་ལ་གཞི་སྣང་གི་དུས་སུ་སྐྱེད་བྱེད་ཀྱི་ནུས་པ་མཐའ་དག་རྫོགས་ནས། སྐུ་དང་ཐིག་ལེ་ཞིང་ཁམས་ཀྱི་བཀོད་པ་སོགས་བསམ་གྱིས་མི་ཁྱབ་པ་འཆར་བས་གཞི་དུས་ཀྱི་འོད་གསལ་དེ་ཉིད་འཆར་གཞིའི་ཚུལ་དུ་ཡོད་པ་དེ་གཞི་སྣང་གི་དུས་སུ་ཡོངས་སུ་རྫོགས་ལ། དེ་ལྟར་ཐོད་རྒལ་གྱི་ལམ་གྱིས་གཏན་ལ་ཕབ་ནས་གོམས་པའི་མཐུས། གཟུགས་སྐུའི་རྣམ་པ་སྒྲུབ་པ་ནི་ལམ་འདིའི་ཁྱད་ཆོས་ཡིན་ནོ། །ཕྱོགས་གླ་མེད་ཀྱི་ལུགས་ཀྱིས་གཞི་ན་ཡོད་པ་ལྟར་ལམ་དུ་བྱེད་པས་ན་དེ་ཉིད་མྱུར་བའང་གནད་དེས་ཡིན་ནོ། །ཕར་ཕྱིན་ཐེག་པ་ལྟར་ན་ལམ་དེ་ལྟར་དུ་བསྒོམ་པའམ། དེ་ལྟར་ལམ་དུ་བྱེད་པའི་ཐབས་མ་བཤད་པའི་རྒྱུ་མཚན་ཤེས་པའང་གལ་ཆེ་གསུང་། རྫོགས་པ་ཆེན་པོ་དང་དུས་འཁོར་གཉིས་ཀྱི་གཟུགས་སྐུ་གཉིས་སྟོང་གཟུགས་ལ་བརྟེན་ནས་བསྒྲུབ་པ་ཙམ་ཞིག་ལ་འདྲ་ན་ཡང་ལམ་གྱི་ཆ་ཐམས་ཅད་ནས་ཐམས་ཅད་དུ་འདྲ་བ་གཏན་མིན་ཏེ། རྫོགས་པ་ཆེན་པོའི་རང་ལམ་ལ་འཆར་གཞི་དང་ལམ་དང་རྩའི་བྱེ་བྲག་སོགས་དང་། ལམ་གྱི་བྱེད་བཅིང་ཐུན་མོང་མ་ཡིན་པ་གཞན་ལས་ལྷག་པའི་ཁྱད་པར་དུ་མ་ཡོད་གསུང་། དུས་འཁོར་དུ་རྟགས་བཅུ་གསུངས་ཀྱང་སྒྲོན་བཞི་དང་སྣང་བཞི་སོགས་མ་གསུང་། རྫོགས་ཆེན་དུ་སྒྲོན་བཞི་སོགས་ཁྱད་པར་དུ་མ་ཞིག་གསུངས་ཀྱང་དུ་བ་ལ་སོགས་པའི་རྟགས་བཅུ་དང་ལམ་གྱི་བྱེད་བཅིང་མང་པོ་མ་གསུངས་པས་སྟོང་གཟུགས་འཆར་ཚུལ་ཙམ་ཞིག་འདྲ་ནའང་ནང་གསེས་ཀྱི་མི་འདྲ་བ་དུ་མ་ཡོད་པ་ནི་ཤེས་སླ་བ་ཡིན་གསུང་། དྲན་རིག་སྣ་ཚོགས་དང་སྣང་བ་སྣ་ཚོགས་བསྐྱེད་པའི་ནུས་པ་རིག་པ་རང་གི་སྟེང་ནས་མ་སད་པའི་གཞི་དུས་ཀྱི་ཆ་དེ་ཉིད་ལམ་ཁྲེགས་ཆོད་ཀྱིས་ཉམས་སུ་ལེན་པ་ནི་གཞི་སྣང་ལམ་དུ་བྱེད་པ་ལ་ལྟོས་ན་ཅུང་ཟད་བུལ་བ་ཡིན་ལ། རིག་པ་རང་གི་དྲན་རིག་དང་སྣང་བ་སྣ་ཚོགས་བསྐྱེད་པའི་ནུས་པ་

སད་པའི་གཞི་སྣང་གི་ཆ་དེ་ཉིད་ལམ་ཐོད་རྒལ་གྱིས་ཉམས་སུ་ལེན་པ་ནི་གཞི་ལམ་དུ་བྱེད་པ་ལ་ལྟོས་ན་ཤིན་ཏུ་མྱུར་བ་ཡིན་པས་དེ་གཉིས་ཀྱི་ཟབ་ཁྱད་ཤེས་པ་འདི་ཉིད་ཀྱང་ལམ་གནད་གལ་ཆེན་ཡིན་ནོ། །ཡར་རྫོགས་པ་ཆེན་པོའི་ལམ་ལ་ལྟོས་ན་སྔགས་བླ་མེད་གཞན་གྱི་ལམ་རྩ་ཐིག་རླུང་གསུམ་ལ་གནད་དུ་བསྣུན་པས་བདེ་ཆེན་གྱི་ཡེ་ཤེས་མཐལ་བར་བྱེད་པའང་རྩུབ་མོའི་སྦྱོར་བ་ཡིན་ཏེ། ཐོག་མར་འོད་གསལ་བདེ་བ་ཆེན་པོའི་ཡེ་ཤེས་མངོན་དུ་གྱུར་པར་བྱེད་པ་ཙམ་ལ་རྩ་རླུང་སོགས་ལ་གནད་དུ་བསྣུན་པའི་ལམ་འདི་ཉིད་ཤིན་ཏུ་མྱུར་ཀྱང་། དེ་ཡང་ཡུན་རིང་མི་བརྟན་པ་སོགས་ཀྱི་སྐྱོན་མང་དུ་ཡོད་དེ། ལམ་འདི་ཉིད་ཡུན་རིང་མོ་ཞིག་གོམས་པར་བྱས་ཏེ་ཐོག་མར་ལམ་རྟགས་ཀྱི་ཡོན་ཏན་རྒྱུད་ལ་སྐྱེས་དགོས་པས་ཀྱང་ཐུང་རིང་ན་ཡང་། གོམས་པའི་ཡེ་ཤེས་རྒྱུད་ལ་སྐྱེས་ཚེ་རྒྱ་ཆེ་ལ་ཡུན་རིང་བ་སོགས་ཀྱི་ཡོན་ཏན་གྱི་ཆ་དུ་མའི་སྒོ་ནས་ལམ་འདི་མྱུར་བ་དང་ཟབ་པས་ཐེག་པའི་རྩེ་རྒྱལ་ཡིན་པ་སོགས་ཀྱི་ཁྱད་ཆོས་མང་པོ་ཞིག་གསུང་ངོ་། །ད་ནི་ཐོད་རྒལ་སྤྱི་ལ་གཅེས་པའི་ཆིངས་སྒྲོན་མ་བཞིའི་རྣམ་བཞག་ཐུང་ཟད་བཤད་ན། རྩ་དབུ་མའི་ནང་དུ་རྒྱུད་སྡེ་གཞན་ལ་མ་གྲགས་པའི་རྩ་ཀ་ཏི་ཤེལ་སྦུག་ཅན་ཞེས་པ་ཁྲག་དང་ཆུ་སེར་གང་གིས་ཀྱང་མ་བསྐྱེད་པའི་མིང་གཞན་རྒྱ་མཚོ་གསེར་གྱི་ཉི་མ་ཡང་ཟེར་ལ་དོན་དུ་དེ་གཉིས་གཅིག་ཡིན་ཏེ། དེ་འདྲའི་རྩ་ཀ་ཏི་ཤེལ་སྦུག་དེ་ཉིད་ཀྱིས་དབུ་མའི་ནང་བརྒྱུད་ནས་སྙིང་ཀ་ནས་ལྟེར་གྱེས་ནས་གཅིག་དབུ་མའི་ནང་བརྒྱུད་དེ་སྤྱི་གཙུག་ཏུ་ཟུག་ལ། གཉིས་མིག་དང་། གཉིས་རྣ་བ་གཉིས་ལ་ཟུག་ནས་ཡོད་པའི་རྩ་དེ་རྣམས་གཅིག་གི་སྒོ་ཕྱེད་ཐུབ་ན་ལྟེ་ཀའི་ཁ་ཕྱེད་ལ། གཅིག་ཁ་ཟུམ་ན་ཀུན་གྱི་ཁ་ཟུམ་ནས་འགྲོ་བ་ཡིན་པས་ཐོག་མར་རྒྱང་ཞགས་ཀྱི་ལམ་གྱི་རྩའི་ཁ་ཕྱེ་བའི་ཐབས་བསྟན་པ་ཡིན་ནོ། །དེ་ནས་སྒྲོན་མ་བཞི་ནི། རྒྱང་ཞགས་ཆུའི་སྒྲོན་མ། དབྱིངས་རྣམ་

དག་གི་སྒྲོན་མ། ཐིག་ལེ་སྟོང་པའི་སྒྲོན་མ། རིག་པ་ལུ་གུ་རྒྱུད་ཀྱི་སྒྲོན་མ་དང་བཞིའོ། །དང་པོ་ནི་མིག་གི་ཨ་འབྲས་ལ་ཟུག་པའི་འོད་རྩ་ཤེལ་སྦུག་ཅན་ཞེས་པ་དེ་ལ་བརྗོད། དེ་ནི་ཁ་ཕྱིར་ཕྱོགས་ནས་ཐ་མལ་གྱི་ས་རྡོ་སོགས་མ་དག་པའི་ཆ་རྣམས་མི་འཛིན་ལ་ཞལ་ནང་དུ་ཕྱོགས་ནས་རིག་པའི་བཞུགས་ཚུལ་གཏིང་གསལ་གཞོན་ནུ་བུམ་སྐུ་བོ་ན་ལ་ཞལ་ཕྱོགས་པ་ཡིན། གཉིས་པ་ནི། དབྱིངས་རྣམ་དག་གི་སྒྲོན་མ་སྟེ་ནམ་མཁའ་གོ་འབྱེད་པའི་ཆ་ནས་ནམ་མཁའི་རང་མདོག་གི་གདངས་སྔོ་རིབ་པའི་རྣམ་པ་དེ་ཡིན། གསུམ་པ་ནི། ཐིག་ལེ་སྟོང་པའི་སྒྲོན་མ་ཉའི་མིག་ལྟ་བུ་འོད་ལྔའི་ཐིག་ལེ་དབུས་མཐིང་ག་ཅན་དེ་ཉིད་ཡིན། བཞི་པ་ནི། རིག་པ་ལུ་གུ་རྒྱུད་ཀྱི་སྒྲོན་མ་ལྕུགས་ཀྱུ་ལྟ་བུའམ། གསེར་གྱི་སྐུད་པ་བཙུ་ཐིག་གི་མདུད་པ་འདྲ་བ་ཐིག་ལེ་དང་ཐིག་ཕྲན་གྱིས་སྤྲེལ་བ་དེ་ཉིད་ཡིན་ལ། དེ་ལ་དབྱེ་ན། ངོ་བོ། རྩལ། གདངས་གསུམ་ལས། དང་པོ་ནི། ཁྲིགས་ཆོད་ཀྱི་རིག་པའམ་རིག་པ་རང་བྱུང་གི་ཡེ་ཤེས་དེ་ཉིད་ཡིན། གཉིས་པ་ནི། ཤེས་རབ་དང་ཏིང་ངེ་འཛིན་དང་གཟུངས་དང་སྤོབས་པ་དང་ཚིག་དོན་ཀློང་རྫོལ་བ་སོགས་དེ་ཉིད་ཡིན། གསུམ་པ་ནི། གདངས་རིག་པ་རྡོ་རྗེ་ལུ་གུ་རྒྱུད་ལྕུགས་ཐག་བསྒྲིལ་བ་ལྟ་བུའམ། བཙུ་ཐིག་གི་མདུད་པ་ལྟ་བུ་དེ་ཉིད་ཡིན། དེ་ལ་ཤེས་རབ་རང་བྱུང་གི་སྒྲོན་མ་ཡང་ཟེར་བ་ཡིན་ནོ། །མཐར་དབྱིངས་རྣམ་དག་གི་སྒྲོན་མ་ཡར་ལྡན་དུ་སོང་བ་ནི་སྣང་རིག་པའི་རྩལ་དབང་གི་སྐབས་སུ་འོག་མིན་སྟུག་པོ་བཀོད་པའི་ཞིང་ཁམས་བཤད་པ་དེ་ཉིད་ཡིན། ཐིག་ལེ་སྟོང་པའི་སྒྲོན་མ་ཡར་ལྡན་དུ་སོང་བ་ནི་ལོངས་སྤྱོད་རྫོགས་སྐུའི་གཞལ་ཡས་ཁང་དུ་གྱུར་པ་དང་། ཤེས་རབ་རང་བྱུང་གི་སྒྲོན་མ་ཡར་ལྡན་དུ་སོང་བ་ནི། སངས་རྒྱས་ལོངས་སྤྱོད་རྫོགས་སྐུར་འགྱུར་བ་དང་། ངོ་བོའམ་རྩལ་ཡར་ལྡན་དུ་སོང་བ་ནི་སངས་རྒྱས་ལོངས་སྤྱོད

རྫོགས་སྐུའི་ཐུགས་རྣམ་པ་ཐམས་ཅད་མཁྱེན་པའི་ཡེ་ཤེས་སུ་འགྱུར་བ་དང་།
ཆོས་ཉིད་ཀྱི་རང་སྒྲ་དེ་ཉིད་ཡར་ལྡན་དུ་སོང་བ་ནི་སངས་རྒྱས་ལོངས་སྤྱོད་རྫོགས་
སྐུའི་གསུང་ཚངས་དབྱངས་ཡན་ལག་དྲུག་ཅུ་གྲུབ་པ་ཡིན་ནོ། །མདོར་ན་
ཁྲེགས་ཆོད་དང་ཐོད་རྒལ་གཉིས་ཀྱི་ལམ་ཉམས་སུ་ལེན་ཚུལ་ཉིད་རྟིལ་གྱིས་དྲིལ་
ན། གཞི་ཀ་དག་དང་ཁྲེགས་ཆོད་ཀྱི་རིག་པའི་བཞུགས་ཚུལ་དེ་ཉིད་འཆི་སྲིད་
ཀྱི་འོད་གསལ་ཁྱད་གཞིར་བྱས་ནས། དེའི་ཁྱད་ཆོས་ཀ་དག་ཟང་ཐལ་རྒྱ་ཡན་
ཡེ་གྲོལ་མ་བཅོས་ཁྱབ་གདལ་གཞོན་ནུ་བུམ་སྐུ་ལ་སོགས་པའི་རིག་པའི་ཁྱད་
ཆོས་དུ་མའི་སྒོ་ནས་དེའི་ཡོན་ཏན་གྱི་ཆ་མི་འདྲ་བ་རེ་རེ་བསྟན་ནས་དེ་ལྟར་བླ་
མའི་མན་ངག་གི་ངོ་སྤྲོད་པའི་དོན་རང་གི་དྲན་པ་ལ་ལེགས་པར་འདྲིས་ངེས་སུ་བྱ།
དེ་ལྟ་བུའི་རིག་པ་དེ་ཉིད་གཞན་ན་ཡོད་པ་མ་ཡིན་ཏེ། ད་ལྟའི་ཤེས་པ་འདི་ཉིད་
ཀྱི་ཆ་གཅིག་བཤད་མ་ཐག་པའི་ཁྱད་ཆོས་དུ་མ་དང་ལྡན་པའི་རིག་པ་ཉིད་ཡིན་
པར་ཐག་གཅིག་ཐོག་དུ་བཅད། བཅད་ཐོག་དེ་ནས་རིག་པའི་བཞུགས་ཚུལ་དེ་
ཉིད་དྲན་པའི་དྲན་པ་ཕྲ་རེ་བ་དེའི་རང་བཞིན་སྐད་ཅིག་ཀྱང་མ་བརྗེད་པར་ད་ལྟའི་
སེམས་འདི་ཉིད་དེའི་ངོ་བོར་གྱུར་སོང་སྙམ་པ་ལྟ་བུའི་མོས་སྒོམ་མ་ཡིན་པར།
ད་ལྟའི་ཤེས་པའི་ཆ་འདི་དག་ཐམས་ཅད་རིག་པ་འདུས་མ་བྱས་ཀྱི་རང་བཞིན་ཁོ་
ན་ཡིན་པར་ཐག་ཆོད་བཞིན་པའི་ངང་ནས་རིག་པའི་བཞུགས་ཚུལ་གྱི་རང་བཞིན་
བསྒོམ་པར་བྱ་བ་ནི་སྐབས་འདིའི་གནད་དོན་ཐུན་མོང་མ་ཡིན་པ་ཡིན་ནོ། །དེ་
ལྟར་མིན་པ་ལ་ཡིན་པར་སྒྲོ་བཏགས་ནས་སྒོམ་པ་ནི་མ་ཡིན་ཏེ། དེ་ལྟར་ཡེ་
ནས་ཡིན་པ་ལ་ཡིན་པ་ལྟར་བླ་མའི་མན་ངག་གིས་ངོ་སྤྲོད་ནས་ལམ་འདིས་སྒོམ་
པར་བྱེད་པ་ཡིན་པར་གོ་བ་འདི་ཡང་གནད་ཀྱི་ཆ་གཅིག་གོ །ཐོད་རྒལ་གྱི་
སྐབས་སུ། རིག་པ་མིག་ལ་གཏད་ཅེས་པའི་དོན་བླ་མེད་ཀྱི་རྒྱུད་སྡེ་གཞན་ལ་
མ་གྲགས་པའི་འོད་རྩ་ཀ་ཏི་ཤེལ་སྦུག་ཅན། རྒྱ་མཚོ་གསེར་གྱི་ཉི་མ་ཞེས་པ་དེ་

ཉིད་རྩ་དབུ་མའི་ནང་དུ་ཡོད་པའི་སྣེ་མིག་གི་ཨ་འབྲས་ཀྱི་དཀྱིལ་དུ་ཐུག་ཚུལ་གྱི་རྡོ་རྗེའི་ལུས་ཀྱི་རྩའི་ཆགས་ཚུལ་དེ་ཐོག་མར་བླ་མའི་མན་ངག་གིས་ངོ་ལེགས་པར་སྤྲོད་པར་བྱས་ནས་ཕྱིས་སུ་རྩ་དེ་ངོ་སྤྲོད་པ་དེ་ལྟར་རང་གི་བློ་ལ་ལེགས་པར་ངེས་པར་བྱས་ནས་དབྱིངས་ཐིག་རིག་གསུམ་གྱི་སྣང་བ་ཐམས་ཅད་རྩ་དེའི་ནང་དུ་ཤར་བ་ཡིན་པ་ལེགས་པར་ཤེས་པར་བྱས་ཏེ། གཞི་ཀ་དག་གི་རིག་པ་མིག་ལ་གཏད། མིག་བར་སྣང་གི་དབྱིངས་རྣམ་དག་གི་སྒྲོན་མ་དང་རིག་པ་ལུ་གུ་རྒྱུད་ལ་གཏད་ནས། དབྱིངས་རིག་ཐིག་གསུམ་གྱི་རྣམ་པ་དེ་ཉིད་རིག་པས་སྐད་ཅིག་ཀྱང་མ་བོར་བར་བསྐྱངས་པ་ནི་ཐོད་རྒལ་གྱི་ལམ་ཐུན་མོང་མ་ཡིན་པ་ཡིན་ཏེ། དེ་ལྟར་འཆར་བར་བྱེད་པ་ལ་ཐོག་མར་ཉི་ཟླ་མར་མེ་གང་རུང་གི་ཡུལ་རྐྱེན་ལ་ལྟོས་ནས་དབྱིངས་ཐིག་གི་སྣང་བ་ལེགས་པར་གོམས་ནས། ཕྱིས་སུ་འོད་རྩ་དེ་ཉིད་སད་ན་ཕྱིས་ཡུལ་རྐྱེན་ལ་མི་ལྟོས་པར་འོད་རྩ་རང་ཉིད་ཀྱི་དབྱིངས་སུ་སྟོང་གཟུགས་ཀྱི་སྣང་བ་བསམ་གྱིས་མི་ཁྱབ་པ་འཆར་བར་བྱེད་པ་ཡིན་ལ། དང་པོར་དེ་ཉིད་ཕྱི་ཡུལ་རྐྱེན་ལ་ལྟོས་དགོས་པ་དང་། དེ་ཉིད་ཡུན་རིང་གོམས་པར་བྱས་ན་ཕྱིའི་ཡུལ་རྐྱེན་ལ་ལྟོས་དགོས་པ་ནི་རྫ་བུམ་མེས་ཚོས་པ་ལྟ་བུའོ། །ཐོད་རྒལ་གྱི་སྐབས་རིག་པ་ཞེས་པ་ནི། རིག་པ་ལུ་གུ་རྒྱུད་ཀྱི་སྒྲོན་མ་དེ་ལ་ངོ་བོ་དང་རྩལ་དང་གདངས་གསུམ་ཡོད་པ་ལ་སྐབས་འདིར་རིག་པ་བརྗོད་པ་ཡིན་ཏེ། ངོ་བོ་སྟོང་ཕྱོགས་ཀྱི་རིག་པ་ཀ་དག་ཁྲེགས་ཆོད་ཀྱི་རིག་པ་ལ་ཟེར། གདངས་སྣང་ཕྱོགས་ཀྱི་རིག་པ་ལྷུན་གྲུབ་ཐོད་རྒལ་གྱི་རིག་པ་རྡོ་རྗེ་ལུ་གུ་རྒྱུད་ལ་ཟེར། རྩལ་རིག་པ་རང་བྱུང་གི་སྒྲོན་མའམ། ཚིག་དོན་གླིང་ནས་རྫོལ་བའི་ཆ་ནས་ཤེས་རབ་རང་བྱུང་གི་སྒྲོན་མ་ཟེར་བ་སོགས་གསུམ་ཀ་ལ་སྐབས་འདིར་རིག་པའི་སྒྲ་འཇུག་པ་ཡིན་གསུང་། སྣང་ཉམས་ཐོད་རྒལ་གྱི་སྣང་ཆ་དང་། ཤེས་ཉམས་ཁྲེགས་ཆོད་ཀྱི་རིག་པ་སྟེ། དེ་

གཉིས་ངོ་བོ་གཅིག་ལ་ལྡོག་པ་ཐ་དད་དུ་ཕྱེ་བ་ཙམ་མ་གཏོགས་ཉི་མ་དང་ཟེར་བཞིན་དུ་ཕན་ཚུན་གཅིག་གྲོགས་སུ་གཅིག་སོང་ནས་སྣང་ཉམས་མཐར་ཕྱུག་སངས་རྒྱས་ཀྱི་གཟུགས་སྐུ་དང་། ཞེས་ཉམས་མཐར་ཕྱུག་སངས་རྒྱས་ཀྱི་ཡེ་ཤེས་ཆོས་སྐུ་སྟེ་དེ་གཉིས་ངོ་བོ་གཅིག་ལ་ལྡོག་ཆའི་བྱེ་བྲག་ཙམ་ཡིན་པ་དཔེར་ན་མེ་དང་ཚ་བ་དང་ཆུ་དང་རླན་བཞིན་ནོ། །ཆོས་ཟད་ཀྱི་སྐབས་སུ་ཕྱིའི་ས་རྡོ་རི་བྲག་ཟད་པ་དང་། ནང་ཕུང་ཁམས་ཟད་པ་དང་། གསང་བ་སེམས་ཀྱི་རྟོགས་ཚོགས་ཟད་པ་དང་། ཡང་གསང་ཐོད་རྒལ་གྱི་སྣང་ཆ་སོགས་ཟད་པའི་ཆོས་ཉིད་ཟད་ས་ཞེས་བརྗོད་དེ། དང་པོ་ནི་ཆོས་ཉིད་ཟད་སར་འཁྱོལ་བའི་རྣལ་འབྱོར་པ་དེས་ལམ་གྱིས་བགྲོད་པ་མཐར་སོན་ནས་མ་དག་པའི་ས་རྡོ་རི་བྲག་སོགས་སྣང་བྱེད་ཀྱི་བག་ཆགས་གཏན་ནས་ཟད་དེ་ཕྱིའི་ཡུལ་གྱི་ས་རྡོ་རི་བྲག་སོགས་ཟད་པ་དང་། གཉིས་པ་ནི་ནང་མ་དག་པའི་ལུས་འདི་སྣང་བྱེད་ཀྱི་བག་ཆགས་གཏན་ནས་ཟད་པས་ནང་ཕུང་ཁམས་ཟད་པ་དང་། གསུམ་པ་ཀུན་རྟོག་ལས་རླུང་གིས་གཡོ་བའི་རྟོག་ཚོགས་སམ་གཟུང་འཛིན་གྱི་སྦྲོས་པ་སྐྱེད་བྱེད་ཀྱི་ནུས་པ་གཏན་ནས་ཟད་པས་གསང་བ་སེམས་ཀྱི་རྟོག་ཚོགས་ཟད་པ་དང་། བཞི་པ་ནི། ལྷུན་གྲུབ་ཐོད་རྒལ་གྱི་སྣང་ཆ་ཐམས་ཅད་གཡོ་བྱེད་ཀྱི་རླུང་ངམ་བག་ཆགས་གཏན་ནས་ཟད་པའི་ཡང་གསང་ཐོད་རྒལ་གྱི་སྣང་ཆ་ཐམས་ཅད་ཟད་པའོ། །སྐབས་འདིར་ཟད་པ་ཞེས་བྱ་བ་ནི་འཁྱོལ་བའི་དོན་ཡིན་པས། ཐོད་རྒལ་གྱི་སྣང་ཆ་ཐམས་ཅད་ཀྱི་རྩལ་ཡོངས་སུ་རྫོགས་པ་འདི་ཉིད་ལས་ལྷག་པ་གཏན་ནས་མེད་ཀྱང་། གཡོ་བྱེད་ཀྱི་རླུང་ལྷག་ལུས་མེད་པར་ཟད་ནས་ལྷུན་གྲུབ་ཐོད་རྒལ་གྱི་སྣང་ཆ་ཐམས་ཅད་ཆོས་ཀྱི་དབྱིངས་སུ་འཁྱོལ་བའམ་རྒྱས་ཐེབས་ཏེ། ཆོས་ཉིད་དེ་བཞིན་ཉིད་ཀྱི་དབྱིངས་ལས་མི་ལྡང་བའི་ཚུལ་དུ་མཉམ་པར་བཞག་བཞིན་གཟུགས་སྐུ་གཉིས་ཀྱིས་གདུལ་བྱའི་སེམས་ཅན་རྣམས་

ཀྱི་འདོད་དོན་གྱི་རེ་བ་ཐམས་ཅད་འབད་མེད་ལྷུན་གྲུབ་ཏུ་སྐོང་ནུས་པའི་གཏེར་མའི་མགོན་པོ་དེ་ཉིད་ལ་ཆོས་ཉིད་ཀྱི་སྒྲས་བསྙད་པའོ། །དེ་ལྟ་བུའི་སྐུ་ཐུགས་ཟུང་དུ་འཇུག་པའི་བསྒྲུབ་བྱ་མཐར་ཐུག་དེ་ཉིད་ནི་རྣམ་པ་གཟུགས་སྐུའི་རོལ་པ་ལ་ངོ་བོ་རྣམ་པ་ཐམས་ཅད་མཁྱེན་པའི་ཡེ་ཤེས་དང་ཟུང་དུ་འཇུག་པའི་གཟུགས་སྐུ་མཐར་ཐུག་གམ་མི་སློབ་ཟུང་འཇུག་གི་སྐུ་གྲུབ་པ་ཡིན་ནོ། །ངོ་བོ་རང་བཞིན་ཐུགས་རྗེ་གསུམ་ནི། ཡེ་གྲོལ་འདུས་མ་བྱས་ཀྱི་རིག་པ་དེ་ཉིད་རང་གི་ངོ་བོ་རང་བཞིན་གྱིས་གྲུབ་པ་རྡུལ་ཙམ་ཡང་མེད་པའི་ཆ་ནས་ངོ་བོ་སྟོང་པར་གསུངས་པ་དང་། འདིར་ནི་ཀུན་རྟོག་ལས་རླུང་གི་གཡོ་བའི་ཆ་གཟུང་འཛིན་གྱི་སྤྲོས་པ་ཐམས་ཅད་དག་ནས་མེད་པའམ་སྟོང་པའི་ཆ་ནས་ངོ་བོ་དང་། རང་བཞིན་གསལ་བ་ནི། གསལ་རིག་གི་ཆ་ཐམས་ཅད་གཏན་ནས་མེད་སོང་བ་ལྟར་མ་ཡིན་པར། རིག་པའི་རང་བཞིན་གསལ་ལ་འགགས་པ་མེད་པ་དྭངས་གསལ་བདེ་བའི་རྣམ་པ་རྒྱུ་གང་དུ་ཡང་མ་ཆད། ཕྱོགས་གང་དུ་ཡང་མ་ལྷུང་བའི་རང་བཞིན་ཅན་ཡིན་ཏེ། དེ་ཡང་རྒྱུ་གང་དུ་ཡང་མ་ཆད་ཅེས་པའང་རིག་པའི་གདངས་དང་ཕྱོགས་ཀྱི་ཆ་ལ་ཚད་བཟུང་དང་བྲལ་བའི་སྟོང་ཁམས་གདལ་བ་ཡིན་པས་རྒྱ་མ་ཆད། རིག་པ་དེ་ཉིད་བདེ་བ་ཁོལ་བུ་དང་སྡུག་བསྔལ་ཁོལ་བུའི་རྣམ་པའི་ཕྱོགས་སུ་ལྷུང་བ་མ་ཡིན་པར་ཀུན་ཁྱབ་གདལ་བ་ཆེན་པོའི་རང་བཞིན་ཡིན་པས་ན་རང་བཞིན་གསལ་བ། ཐུགས་རྗེ་ཀུན་ཁྱབ་ཞེས་པ་ནི། སྤྱིར་ཐུགས་རྗེ་ཞེས་པ་སྙིང་རྗེ་ལ་བཤད་ཀྱང་། སྐབས་འདིར་ནི་རིག་པ་བརྟན་གཡོ་སྣོད་བཅུད་དང་བཅས་པའི་འཆར་གཞིར་གྱུར་པ་ཡིན་ཏེ། དེ་ཐམས་ཅད་རིག་པའི་རྩལ་དང་། རིག་པའི་རྣམ་འཕྲུལ་ལམ། ཆོ་འཕྲུལ་ཡིན་པར་ཤེས་དགོས། འཁོར་འདས་གཉིས་ལ་མ་ཁྱབ་པ་མེད་ཅིང་འཁོར་འདས་གཉིས་ཀྱི་སྒྲོག་འཛིན་ཅིང་། འདི་ཡོད་མེད་ཀྱི་རྗེས་སུ་འགྲོ་ལྡོག་བྱེད་པས་

ཐུགས་རྗེ་ཀུན་ལ་ཁྱབ་པའོ། ། འདི་ནི་རྗེ་བླ་མ་ཉིད་སྐུ་ན་གཞོན་དུས་འགའ་ཞིག་ལ་གསུང་རིམ་བཞིན་ཟིན་ཐོར་བཏབ་པ་ཡིན་ཀྱང་དེང་དུས་ཀྱི་གསུང་སྒྲོས་དང་མི་མཐུན་ཞིང་དཔེ་ཡང་དག་མོ་ཞིག་གཏན་མ་རྙེད་ཀྱང་རྗེ་བླ་མ་ཉིད་ལ་ཞུས་པ་ལྟར་གང་ཤེས་ཀྱིས་ཞུ་དག་བྱས་ནས་སྦྱར་ལ་བཏབ་པའོ།། ...ཤིང་པར་གྱི་མཆན།། ||

INDEX